Clan 6MT Pacific' 72003 'Clan Fraser' prepares to leave Princes Street with an express for Glasgow Central.

RAILWAY DIS
ILLUSTRA
EDINBUR
(PRINCES STREET).

Even at the height of its activity, the Caledonian/LMS tended to be overlooked at Edinburgh which - given the scale of operations around the Waverley - gave the impression that the city was a North British monopoly: a perception understandable if not entirely just.

Few of the operational complexities that characterised the North British were present at Princes Street where the system comprised a main line to Glasgow Central with a divergence to Carstairs at Midcalder Junction, eleven miles out of Edinburgh. The service consisted of eleven trains from Edinburgh to Glasgow and fourteen departures for Carstairs, some of the latter being extended to Muirkirk, Lanark or Symington.

Thanks to the complex cyclic diagrams beloved of the London Midland, the class 5 4-6-0's booked to most of the Glasgow trains were frequently replaced by engines that were remarkable by any standards. To sample a run behind a Stanier Pacific passengers from Euston had to select the most prestigious trains in the timetable yet in Scotland the same end could be achieved by boarding a three-coach suburban formations from Glasgow Central to Edinburgh Princes Street.

In prewar years most of the West Coast Anglo-Scottish trains had included Edinburgh portions and although the East Coast became the favoured route for Edinburgh after 1939, Prices Street continued to provide through facilities albeit on a reduced scale.

There were however some surprises and the chief of these was the fact that through coaches to (but not from) Euston operated every night although they were only advertised in the public timetable as running to Crewe. The train concerned was the 17.35 from Princes Street which by-passed Carstairs and ran to Symington where it transferred two vehicles to the 17.40 Glasgow Central - Euston. In spite of

GRADIENT CHART		
m. ch	Station	1 in
0.00	GLASGOW CENTRAL	-
1.01	Eglinton Street	-345
3.13	Rutherglen	669
5.03	Cambuslang	261
6.50	Newton	204
8.37	Uddingston	-345
10.76	Bellshill	76
13.06	HOLYTOWN	163
13.69	Carfin	120
15.52	Cleland	130
18.59	Hartwood	96
20.36	SHOTTS	108
23.01	Benhar Jcn	128
23.66	Fauldhouse North	-104
26.01	Breich	-197
28.52	Addiewell	-176
30.24	Westcalder	-146
32.23	New Park	-270
34.73	Midcalder Jcn	347
36.08	Midcalder	-138
43.16	Kingsknowe	-165
44.00	Slateford	-115
45.00	Merchiston	-195
46.16	EDINBURGH (P. ST)	-1629

Cont. Page 21

Prior to 1939 there had been a certain amount of competition between the LMS and LNER for passenger traffic between Glasgow and Edinburgh with little to choose between the trains of either company. Both provided restaurant cars - Pullman cars in some services - and accomplished the journey in 60 to 70 minutes depending on the number of stops.   After the war however the North British line was nominated as the principal route and although competition from the Caledonian service waned, not all the Princes Street services degenerated into stopping trains.   During the 1950's several services ran from Glasgow Central to Princes Street in under 80 minutes; the fastest being the 08.40 from Glasgow which reached Edinburgh in 73 minutes.

Although booked to 5MT 4-6-0's, the locomotive Inspectors at Central frequently had to improvise on the booked diagrams and not infrequently arranged for Stanier Pacifics to make a return trip to Edinburgh in order to ease the shortage of smaller engines.

On 31st May 1958 greater piquancy was added to the spectacle of a Coronation Pacific on a Glasgow train by the fact that the engine was a Camden-based member of the class and unusual under any circumstances north of Carlisle. 46245 'City of London' recently repainted in maroon livery approaches Merchiston with an Edinburgh - Glasgow express.

Although Polmadie was well supplied with express passenger engines - in early 1951 it possessed 5 Jubilee 4-6-0's, 5 Royal Scot 4-6-0's and 12 class 8 Pacifics - it had only nine 5MT 4-6-0's which at times left the shed very short of medium-distance passenger engines. Several of the Coronation Pacific turns, however, called for nothing more strenuous than a return trip to Carlisle and to alleviate 5MT shortages, the Motive Power Inspectors at Glasgow Central would often utilise a Pacific for a trip to Princes Street and back. The 08.40 from Glasgow Central - an express on a booking of 73 minutes with stops at Holytown and Shotts - was a regular turn for a Pacific that had earlier arrived in the Central with an overnight Anglo-Scottish service and although the arrangement went a long way to ensuring a punctual arrival in Edinburgh, the return working produced the curious spectacle of a Coronation Pacific at the head of three non-corridor coaches and making eighteen stops in forty-six miles. Polmadie-based 46220 'Coronation' was caught in the working on the 5th February 1955 as it passed Slateford with the 11.37 Edinburgh - Glasgow. The engine is in its 'intermediate' semi-streamlined condition; the sloping smokebox being a reminder of the days when it was fully streamlined. A Caledonian route-indicator - a complete list of the positions is given on page 36 - is displayed on the off-side lamp bracket.

The distinction between a class A (Express) service and a class B was not always easy to determine. Some of the Edinburgh - Glasgow trains called at almost all stations and were justly classified as class B services yet the 13.30 Edinburgh to Glasgow which called at no less than eight intermediate stations was acccorded the open lights of an express. Coronation Pacific 46232 'Duchess of Montrose' stands at the head of the 13.30 to Glasgow Central at Princes Street on the 6th April 1955.

Coronation 8P 46232 'Duchess of Montrose' pulls away from Princes Street with the 13.30 Edinburgh to Glasgow Central on 6th April 1955.

ENGINE MOVEMENTS: Given that it represented London Midland (Caledonian) interests in the Capital, Dalry Road's allocation of only 44 engines seemed rather trifling especially when compared with the 300 engines shared between Haymarket and St Margaret's.

Much of Dalry Road's attraction lay in the fact it was an LMS ghetto in the midst of an LNER environment and engines that would scarcely have attracted a glance elsewhere became, in Edinburgh, a focus of novelty.

While Princes Street retained a small share of West Coast business, the Edinburgh sections ran independently only over the 30-odd miles to Symington and this militated against the allocation of any large express engines at Dalry Road. In fact the largest engines available at Edinburgh for this type of work were the LMS 5MT 4-6-0's although 4-4-0's (Compounds and ex Caledonian) were often to be found on the lighter of the workings. Generally the 4-6-0's were to be found on the iron-ore trains between Crew Junction, Leith, and the various steel works in the Glasgow area and it was surprising to find that in early 1951, the shed was almost denuded of 4-6-0's as the diagramming for the iron-ore workings was transferred - temporarily - to sheds in the Glasgow area. The remaining class 5 work was covered by a trio of 'Crab' 2-6-0's, a pair of J37 0-6-0's, 45022 and - rather surprisingly - a pair of LNER B1 4-6-0's which, with a third J37, arrived from St Margaret's in the Spring of 1951.

This was a highly interesting development since in England the regions were effectively the former railway companies under a different name whilst in Scotland the LNER and LMS had been merged into a single body. The question of the hour concerned the

Loco	Class	ENGINE ALLOCATION & TRANSFERS : EDINBURGH (DALRY ROAD)											
		Aug-50	Sep-50	Oct-50	Nov-50	Dec-50	Jan-51	Feb-51	Mar-51	Apr-51	May-51	Jun-51	Jul-51
61002	5MT: B1 4-6-0 (1942)	X	X	X	X	X	X	X	Ex E'burgh(SM)				
61242	5MT: B1 4-6-0 (1942)	X	X	X	X	X	X	X	X	Ex E'burgh(SM)			
45022	5MT 4-6-0 (1934)												
45023	5MT 4-6-0 (1934)								To Polmadie	X	X	X	X
45029	5MT 4-6-0 (1934)									To M'well	X	X	X
45036	5MT 4-6-0 (1934)	X	X	X	Ex E'burgh(SM)	To Polmadie	X	X	X	X	X	X	X
45085	5MT 4-6-0 (1934)	X	X	X	Ex E'burgh(SM)				To Polmadie	X	X	X	X
45184	5MT 4-6-0 (1934)									To Upperby	X	X	
45362	5MT 4-6-0 (1934)									To Cork'll	X	X	X
42804	5MT 2-6-0 (1926)												
42807	5MT 2-6-0 (1926)												
42830	5MT 2-6-0 (1926)												
64536	5F: J37 0-6-0 (1914)												
64547	5F: J37 0-6-0 (1914)	X	X	X	X	X	X	X	X	X	Ex E'burgh(SM)		
64591	5F: J37 0-6-0 (1914)												
40911	4P 4-4-0 (1924)												
41177	4P 4-4-0 (1924)												
41178	4P 4-4-0 (1924)												
42268	4MT 2-6-4T (1945)												
42269	4MT 2-6-4T (1945)												
42270	4MT 2-6-4T (1945)												
42271	4MT 2-6-4T (1945)												
42272	4MT 2-6-4T (1945)												
42273	4MT 2-6-4T (1945)												
54478	3P 4-4-0 (1920)												
54451	3P 4-4-0 (1910)												
54452	3P 4-4-0 (1910)												
69187	3F: N15 0-6-2T (1910)												
56253	3F 0-6-0T (1896)												
56283	3F 0-6-0T (1896)												
56312	3F 0-6-0T (1896)												
56313	3F 0-6-0T (1896)												
57654	3F 0-6-0 (1918)												
57550	3F 0-6-0 (1899)												
57553	3F 0-6-0 (1899)												
57559	3F 0-6-0 (1899)												
57565	3F 0-6-0 (1899)												
57576	3F 0-6-0 (1899)												
57645	3F 0-6-0 (1899)												
55165	2P 0-4-4T (1900)												
55166	2P 0-4-4T (1900)												
55177	2P 0-4-4T (1900)												
55189	2P 0-4-4T (1900)												
55202	2P 0-4-4T (1900)												
55210	2P 0-4-4T (1900)												
55229	2P 0-4-4T (1900)												
55233	2P 0-4-4T (1900)	X	Ex Beattock										
55139	2P 0-4-4T (1895)												
65271	2F: J36 0-6-0 (1888)												
65311	2F: J36 0-6-0 (1888)	X	X	X	X	X	X	X	X	X	Ex E'burgh(SM)		
47163	2F 0-6-0T (1928)												

extent to which the merger would see a blurring of pre-1948 differences and the transfer of 61002 and 61242 seemed to suggest that locomotives were being treated as common property; a trend that had started on the West Highland where many of the LNER 2-6-0 workings had been taken over by Black 5 4-6-0's.

It was not a prospect that appealed to the conservative element - A1 and A4 pacifics were already being operated between Glasgow Central and Crewe - and one wondered, rather unhappily, where it would all end.

So far as Dalry Road was concerned the crisis of identity was short-lived and in the Autumn of 1951 the two LNER 4-6-0's returned to their native metals as LMS Black 5's came back in respectable numbers.

Once the early euphoria of a merged railway had died down and its more adventurous spirits reminded that they had more profitable things to do than introduce change for its own sake, the two elements continued more or less as they had always done.

There were instances of LMS engines running over LNER routes but usually it emanated from the grey areas of Perth or Aberdeen where the two organisations shared common facilities. The latter provided engines for both the Perth and Dundee expresses and it only required a single failure of an LMS Black 5 to see an LNER V2 2-6-2 working over the Caledonian to Perth and then - if the motive power position remained

Loco	Class	Aug-51	Sep-51	Oct-51	Nov-51	Dec-51	Jan-52	Feb-52	Mar-52	Apr-52	May-52	Jun-52	Jul-52
				ENGINE ALLOCATION & TRANSFERS : EDINBURGH (DALRY ROAD)									
61002	5MT: B1 4-6-0 (1942)		To Darlington	X	X	X	X	X	X	X	X	X	X
61242	5MT: B1 4-6-0 (1942)			To Keith	X	X	X	X	X	X	X	X	X
44994	5MT 4-6-0 (1934)	X	X	X	X	X	X	X	X	Ex Kingmoor			
45022	5MT 4-6-0 (1934)												
45023	5MT 4-6-0 (1934)	X	X	Ex Polmadie									
45086	5MT 4-6-0 (1934)	X	X	Ex Carstairs									
45127	5MT 4-6-0 (1934)	X	Ex Perth										
45161	5MT 4-6-0 (1934)	X	X	Ex Carstairs									
45183	5MT 4-6-0 (1934)	X	X	Ex Shrewsbury									
42804	5MT 2-6-0 (1926)												
42807	5MT 2-6-0 (1926)												
42830	5MT 2-6-0 (1926)												
64536	5F: J37 0-6-0 (1914)												
64547	5F: J37 0-6-0 (1914)												
64591	5F: J37 0-6-0 (1914)												
40911	4P 4-4-0 (1924)												
41177	4P 4-4-0 (1924)												
41178	4P 4-4-0 (1924)												
42268	4MT 2-6-4T (1945)												
42269	4MT 2-6-4T (1945)												
42270	4MT 2-6-4T (1945)												
42271	4MT 2-6-4T (1945)												
42272	4MT 2-6-4T (1945)												
42273	4MT 2-6-4T (1945)												
54478	3P 4-4-0 (1920)												
54451	3P 4-4-0 (1910)												
54452	3P 4-4-0 (1910)												
69187	3F: N15 0-6-2T (1910)												
56253	3F 0-6-0T (1896)												
56283	3F 0-6-0T (1896)												
56312	3F 0-6-0T (1896)												
56313	3F 0-6-0T (1896)												
57654	3F 0-6-0 (1918)			W/D	X	X	X	X	X	X	X	X	X
57550	3F 0-6-0 (1899)												
57553	3F 0-6-0 (1899)												
57559	3F 0-6-0 (1899)												
57565	3F 0-6-0 (1899)												
57576	3F 0-6-0 (1899)												
57645	3F 0-6-0 (1899)												
55165	2P 0-4-4T (1900)												
55166	2P 0-4-4T (1900)												
55177	2P 0-4-4T (1900)												
55189	2P 0-4-4T (1900)												To Polmadie
55202	2P 0-4-4T (1900)												
55210	2P 0-4-4T (1900)												
55229	2P 0-4-4T (1900)												
55233	2P 0-4-4T (1900)												
55139	2P 0-4-4T (1895)												
65271	2F: J36 0-6-0 (1888)												
65311	2F: J36 0-6-0 (1888)												
47163	2F 0-6-0T (1928)												

critical - south to either Buchanan Street or Carlisle).

The departure of the B1's was not the end of Dalry Road's association with LNER locomotives although those that remained tended to be at the smaller end of the scale: a couple of J36 0-6-0's, three J37 0-6-0's and an N15 0-6-2T for Edinburgh suburban trip work. Most of these transfers had arisen from a shortage of power caused by the condition of some of the ex-Caledonian 0-6-0's; the J37's being diagrammed to the 00.50 Slateford Yard to Mossend and the 04.20 return. In extremis during 1951 and 1952, C16 4-4-2T's appeared on loan from St Margaret's to assist with the Kingsknowe and Leith workings.

1953 and 1954 were relatively stable years so far as the Dalry Road allocation went and the only movements of note was the arrival of two more J35 0-6-0's from St Margarets - bringing the total up to four - because of the continuing poor condition of the Caledonian engines. One interesting incident during this period was the unannounced arrival of brand-new BR 3MT 2-6-0 77011 for which no diagrams had been issued. It transpired that several of the class had been allocated to Polmadie and because of this someone had assumed that 77011 was intended for Dalry Road when in actual fact the engine should have

Loco	Class	Aug-52	Sep-52	Oct-52	Nov-52	Dec-52	Jan-53	Feb-53	Mar-53	Apr-53	May-53	Jun-53	Jul-53
	ENGINE ALLOCATION & TRANSFERS : EDINBURGH (DALRY ROAD)												
44994	5MT 4-6-0 (1934)							To E'burgh (SM)	X	X	X	X	Ex E'burgh (SM)
45022	5MT 4-6-0 (1934)												
45023	5MT 4-6-0 (1934)												
45086	5MT 4-6-0 (1934)												
45127	5MT 4-6-0 (1934)												
45161	5MT 4-6-0 (1934)												
45183	5MT 4-6-0 (1934)												
42804	5MT 2-6-0 (1926)												
42807	5MT 2-6-0 (1926)												
42830	5MT 2-6-0 (1926)												
64536	5F: J37 0-6-0 (1914)												
64547	5F: J37 0-6-0 (1914)				To E'burgh (SM)	X	X	X	X	X	X	X	X
64591	5F: J37 0-6-0 (1914)												
40911	4P 4-4-0 (1924)					W/D	X	X	X	X	X	X	X
41147	4P 4-4-0 (1924)	X	X	X	X	Ex Carstairs							
41177	4P 4-4-0 (1924)												
41178	4P 4-4-0 (1924)												
42268	4MT 2-6-4T (1945)												
42269	4MT 2-6-4T (1945)												
42270	4MT 2-6-4T (1945)												
42271	4MT 2-6-4T (1945)												
42272	4MT 2-6-4T (1945)												
42273	4MT 2-6-4T (1945)												
54478	3P 4-4-0 (1920)												
54451	3P 4-4-0 (1910)												
54452	3P 4-4-0 (1910)												
69187	3F: N15 0-6-2T (1910)												
64495	3F: J35 0-6-0 (1906)	X	X	X	X	Ex Thornton Jn							
64500	3F: J35 0-6-0 (1906)	X	X	X	X	Ex Thornton Jn							
56253	3F 0-6-0T (1896)												
56283	3F 0-6-0T (1896)												
56312	3F 0-6-0T (1896)												
56313	3F 0-6-0T (1896)												
57679	3F 0-6-0 (1918)	X	X	Ex Carstairs									
57550	3F 0-6-0 (1899)												
57553	3F 0-6-0 (1899)					To Polmadie	X	X	X	X	X	X	X
57559	3F 0-6-0 (1899)												
57565	3F 0-6-0 (1899)												
57576	3F 0-6-0 (1899)												
57603	3F 0-6-0 (1899)	X	X	Ex Carstairs		To Polmadie	X	X	X	X	X	X	X
57645	3F 0-6-0 (1899)												
55165	2P 0-4-4T (1900)												
55166	2P 0-4-4T (1900)												
55177	2P 0-4-4T (1900)												
55202	2P 0-4-4T (1900)												
55210	2P 0-4-4T (1900)												
55229	2P 0-4-4T (1900)												
55233	2P 0-4-4T (1900)												
55139	2P 0-4-4T (1895)	W/D	X	X	X	X	X	X	X	X	X	X	X
65271	2F: J36 0-6-0 (1888)	W/D	X	X	X	X	X	X	X	X	X	X	X
65311	2F: J36 0-6-0 (1888)				To E'burgh (SM)	X	X	X	X	X	X	X	X
47163	2F 0-6-0T (1928)												

been sent to Darlington.

Withdrawals were few in number but whilst the departure of the aging 55166 came as no surprise, the loss of an LMS compound - not thirty years old and no more venerable than many of the four-coupled passenger engines across the way at the Waverley - caused a few eyebrows to rise.

By way of balancing the books in the face of the LNER engines at work on the Caledonian, one of the compound diagrams cut a swathe through North British territory. The service was a survivor of pre-grouping times when running powers had been conceded by the North British in order to allow Caledonian services from Princes Street to have access to their own lines north of the Clyde Valley. The route followed was over the connection between Dalry Road and Haymarket and then over the NBR main line to Falkirk Grahamstone, returning to Caledonian metals at Larbert. Although appearing as something of an anachronism, in fact the

Loco	Class	Aug-53	Sep-53	Oct-53	Nov-53	Dec-53	Jan-54	Feb-54	Mar-54	Apr-54	May-54	Jun-54	Jul-54
	ENGINE ALLOCATION & TRANSFERS : EDINBURGH (DALRY ROAD)												
44994	5MT 4-6-0 (1934)												
45022	5MT 4-6-0 (1934)												
45023	5MT 4-6-0 (1934)												
45086	5MT 4-6-0 (1934)												
45127	5MT 4-6-0 (1934)												
45161	5MT 4-6-0 (1934)												
45183	5MT 4-6-0 (1934)												
42804	5MT 2-6-0 (1926)												
42807	5MT 2-6-0 (1926)												
42830	5MT 2-6-0 (1926)												
64536	5F:J37 0-6-0 (1914)												
64591	5F:J37 0-6-0 (1914)												
41147	4P 4-4-0 (1924)												
41177	4P 4-4-0 (1924)												
41178	4P 4-4-0 (1924)					W/D	X	X	X	X	X	X	X
42268	4MT 2-6-4T (1945)												
42269	4MT 2-6-4T (1945)												
42270	4MT 2-6-4T (1945)												
42271	4MT 2-6-4T (1945)												
42272	4MT 2-6-4T (1945)												
42273	4MT 2-6-4T (1945)												
54478	3P 4-4-0 (1920)												
54451	3P 4-4-0 (1910)												
54452	3P 4-4-0 (1910)												
69187	3F: N15 0-6-2T (1910)												
64495	3F:J35 0-6-0 (1906)												
64500	3F:J35 0-6-0 (1906)												
64517	3F:J35 0-6-0 (1906)	X	X	X	X	X	X	X	X	X	Ex E'burgh (SM)		
64527	3F:J35 0-6-0 (1906)	X	X	X	X	X	X	X	X	X	Ex E'burgh (SM)		
56253	3F 0-6-0T (1896)												
56283	3F 0-6-0T (1896)												
56312	3F 0-6-0T (1896)												
56313	3F 0-6-0T (1896)												
57679	3F 0-6-0 (1918)												
57550	3F 0-6-0 (1899)												
57559	3F 0-6-0 (1899)												
57565	3F 0-6-0 (1899)												
57576	3F 0-6-0 (1899)												
57645	3F 0-6-0 (1899)												
55165	2P 0-4-4T (1900)												
55166	2P 0-4-4T (1900)		W/D	X	X	X	X	X	X	X	X	X	X
55177	2P 0-4-4T (1900)												
55202	2P 0-4-4T (1900)												
55210	2P 0-4-4T (1900)												
55229	2P 0-4-4T (1900)												
55233	2P 0-4-4T (1900)												
47163	2F 0-6-0T (1928)												

service survived because it was the most direct way of travelling between Edinburgh and Stirling.

There were seven of these departures - neither the grouping nor nationalisation affected them greatly - from Princes Street, four to Stirling, one to Callender and two to Perth; the last-mentioned being a duty for a Dalry Road Compound. 41147 and 41177 were the regular engines for the 09.35 service and it was pleasant to fly through stations such as Polmont and Linlithgow behind either an LMS 4-4-0 or 2-6-4T. (It was, however, possible to be caught out. For the workings operated from the other end of the line, Stirling would often use a North British 4-4-0: D30 62426).

The latter part of 1955 saw a number of changes which helped to diminish the pregrouping element at Dalry Road.

In September the shed's remaining Compound 4-4-0's, 41147 and 41177, were sent to Stranraer as replacements for engines that had been taken out of traffic, their place on the Perth trains being taken by 5MT 4-6-0's.

The trio of Horwich

Loco	Class	Aug-54	Sep-54	Oct-54	Nov-54	Dec-54	Jan-55	Feb-55	Mar-55	Apr-55	May-55	Jun-55	Jul-55
	ENGINE ALLOCATION & TRANSFERS : EDINBURGH (DALRY ROAD)												
44994	5MT 4-6-0 (1934)												
45022	5MT 4-6-0 (1934)												
45023	5MT 4-6-0 (1934)												
45086	5MT 4-6-0 (1934)												
45127	5MT 4-6-0 (1934)												
45161	5MT 4-6-0 (1934)												
45183	5MT 4-6-0 (1934)												
42804	5MT 2-6-0 (1926)												
42807	5MT 2-6-0 (1926)												
42830	5MT 2-6-0 (1926)												
64536	5F: J37 0-6-0 (1914)												
64591	5F: J37 0-6-0 (1914)												
41147	4P 4-4-0 (1924)												
41177	4P 4-4-0 (1924)												
42268	4MT 2-6-4T (1945)												
42269	4MT 2-6-4T (1945)												
42270	4MT 2-6-4T (1945)												
42271	4MT 2-6-4T (1945)												
42272	4MT 2-6-4T (1945)												
42273	4MT 2-6-4T (1945)												
42695	4MT 2-6-4T (1945)	X	X	X	X	X	Ex Polmadie						
54478	3P 4-4-0 (1920)												
54451	3P 4-4-0 (1910)												
54452	3P 4-4-0 (1910)												
69187	3F: N15 0-6-2T (1910)												
64495	3F: J35 0-6-0 (1906)												
64500	3F: J35 0-6-0 (1906)												
64517	3F: J35 0-6-0 (1906)												
64527	3F: J35 0-6-0 (1906)												
64528	3F: J35 0-6-0 (1906)	X	X	X	X	X	X	X	X	X	Ex Polmont		
56253	3F 0-6-0T (1896)												
56283	3F 0-6-0T (1896)												
56312	3F 0-6-0T (1896)												
56313	3F 0-6-0T (1896)												
57679	3F 0-6-0 (1918)												
57550	3F 0-6-0 (1899)												
57559	3F 0-6-0 (1899)												
57565	3F 0-6-0 (1899)												
57576	3F 0-6-0 (1899)											To Oban	X	X
57645	3F 0-6-0 (1899)												
55165	2P 0-4-4T (1900)												
55177	2P 0-4-4T (1900)											W/D		X
55202	2P 0-4-4T (1900)												
55210	2P 0-4-4T (1900)												
55229	2P 0-4-4T (1900)												
55233	2P 0-4-4T (1900)												
47163	2F 0-6-0T (1928)												

5MT 2-6-0's which had worked the night express goods to and from Carlisle were transferred to Kingmoor in exchange for two Black Fives from Corkerhill.

The sum of these movements together with the introduction of a night goods service to Stranraer was to leave the depot short to the tune of two class 4 engines; a deficit that was eased in early 1956 by the reappearance of B1 4-6-0's at the shed after an absence of five years.

Like their predecessors, the newcomers did not remain long at Dalry Road - 61407 went to Dunfermline in April 1957 whilst 61246 returned to St Margarets at the beginning of 1958 - but their appearance seems to have acted as a signal for an increase in North British influence with three of the large North British J37 0-6-0's coming from Dunfermline in the autumn of 1956 to add to the trio already at Dalry Road. (These, together with the J35 0-6-0's whose numbers had increased rather quietly over the years, could give the shed quite an LNER flavour at times).

After taking receipt of the J37's, the shed once again settled down with the only alterations of significance being the exchange of 61407 for 45007 and the departure of 4MT 42269 to Aviemore - a move which broke the numerically nice block allocation of LMS tanks at Dalry Road. To maintain numbers, a Caledonian 3F 0-6-0 was received from Corkerhill.

		ENGINE ALLOCATION & TRANSFERS : EDINBURGH (DALRY ROAD)											
Loco	Class	Aug-55	Sep-55	Oct-55	Nov-55	Dec-55	Jan-56	Feb-56	Mar-56	Apr-56	May-56	Jun-56	Jul-56
61246	5MT: B1 4-6-0 (1942)	X	X	X	X	X	X	Ex E'burgh (SM)					
61407	5MT: B1 4-6-0 (1942)	X	X	X	X	X	X	Ex E'burgh (SM)					
44994	5MT 4-6-0 (1934)												
45022	5MT 4-6-0 (1934)												
45023	5MT 4-6-0 (1934)												
45030	5MT 4-6-0 (1934)	X	X	Ex Corkerhill									
45036	5MT 4-6-0 (1934)	X	X	Ex Corkerhill									
45086	5MT 4-6-0 (1934)												
45127	5MT 4-6-0 (1934)												
45161	5MT 4-6-0 (1934)												
45183	5MT 4-6-0 (1934)												
42804	5MT 2-6-0 (1926)			To Kingmoor	X	X	X	X	X	X	X	X	X
42807	5MT 2-6-0 (1926)												
42830	5MT 2-6-0 (1926)			To Kingmoor	X	X	X	X	X	X	X	X	X
64536	5F: J37 0-6-0 (1914)												
64591	5F: J37 0-6-0 (1914)												
64612	5F: J37 0-6-0 (1914)	X	X	X	X	X	X	X	X	Ex Carstairs			
41147	4P 4-4-0 (1924)		To Stranraer	X	X	X	X	X	X	X	X	X	X
41177	4P 4-4-0 (1924)		To Stranraer	X	X	X	X	X	X	X	X	X	X
42268	4MT 2-6-4T (1945)												
42269	4MT 2-6-4T (1945)												
42270	4MT 2-6-4T (1945)												
42271	4MT 2-6-4T (1945)												
42272	4MT 2-6-4T (1945)												
42273	4MT 2-6-4T (1945)												
42695	4MT 2-6-4T (1945)												
54478	3P 4-4-0 (1920)												
54451	3P 4-4-0 (1910)		W/D	X	X	X	X	X	X	X	X	X	X
54452	3P 4-4-0 (1910)												
69187	3F: N15 0-6-2T (1910)												
64495	3F: J35 0-6-0 (1906)												
64500	3F: J35 0-6-0 (1906)												
64517	3F: J35 0-6-0 (1906)												
64527	3F: J35 0-6-0 (1906)												
64528	3F: J35 0-6-0 (1906)		To Polmont	X	X	X	X	X	X	X	X	X	X
56253	3F 0-6-0T (1896)												
56283	3F 0-6-0T (1896)												
56312	3F 0-6-0T (1896)												
56313	3F 0-6-0T (1896)												
57679	3F 0-6-0 (1918)												
57550	3F 0-6-0 (1899)												
57559	3F 0-6-0 (1899)												
57565	3F 0-6-0 (1899)												
57576	3F 0-6-0 (1899)	Ex Oban											
57645	3F 0-6-0 (1899)												
55165	2P 0-4-4T (1900)												
55202	2P 0-4-4T (1900)												
55210	2P 0-4-4T (1900)												
55229	2P 0-4-4T (1900)												
55233	2P 0-4-4T (1900)												
47163	2F 0-6-0T (1928)												

Amongst the more venerable of Dalry Road's engines were three Caledonian 4-4-0's, one of which could occasionally be found on the Symington workings. One of the engines - 54452 - was one of the celebrated Superheated Dunalastair IV's of 1910 - whilst the others were later (1920) versions of the same design.

Much to the satisfaction and surprise of many observers - and probably several of the staff - it began to look as though the Caledonian 4-4-0's were going to outlast the Standard Compounds; the latter still being viewed by many as something of an invader. One of the Dunalastair IV's was taken out of traffic at the same time as the Compounds departed to Stranraer but the others soldiered on until the end of the 1957 summer period when 54452 was withdrawn from service leaving 54478, one of the improved Dunalastairs of 1920, as the only Caledonian 4-4-0 at the shed. Interestingly 54452 went without being replaced.

Amongst the reasons that the Caledonian 4-4-0's were retained in favour of the Compounds was that the area had a heavy bias towards goods traffic for which the Compounds, being prohibited from working unfitted services, were not suited.

In early 1958 B1 4-6-0 61248 was sent back to St Margaret's in exchange for Black 5 45155 of Haymarket and for a moment it appeared that LMS influence had won the day at least so far as passenger operations were concerned.

The moment was a brief one since in May 1958 - without warning - the Caledonian 0-4-4T's which had maintained passenger services between Princes Street and Leith for almost as long as anyone could remember were usurped by diesel multiple-units. To add insult to injury, the service was increased from fourteen to twenty-seven workings in each direction and a substantial increase in patronage declared. The point that the 0-4-4T's could also have increased usage by doubling their mileage but without the capital costs of dieselisation was not mentioned.

The new multiple units were a symbol of

Loco	Class	Aug-56	Sep-56	Oct-56	Nov-56	Dec-56	Jan-57	Feb-57	Mar-57	Apr-57	May-57	Jun-57	Jul-57
61246	5MT: B1 4-6-0 (1942)												
61407	5MT: B1 4-6-0 (1942)									To Dunfermline	X	X	X
44994	5MT 4-6-0 (1934)												
45007	5MT 4-6-0 (1934)	X	X	X	X	X	X	X	X	X	X	Ex Kingmoor	
45022	5MT 4-6-0 (1934)												
45023	5MT 4-6-0 (1934)												
45030	5MT 4-6-0 (1934)												
45036	5MT 4-6-0 (1934)												
45086	5MT 4-6-0 (1934)												
45127	5MT 4-6-0 (1934)												
45161	5MT 4-6-0 (1934)												
45183	5MT 4-6-0 (1934)												
42807	5MT 2-6-0 (1926)												
64536	5F: J37 0-6-0 (1914)												
64554	5F: J37 0-6-0 (1914)	X	Ex Dunfermline										
64561	5F: J37 0-6-0 (1914)	X	Ex Dunfermline										
64574	5F: J37 0-6-0 (1914)	X	Ex Dunfermline										
64591	5F: J37 0-6-0 (1914)												
64612	5F: J37 0-6-0 (1914)												
42268	4MT 2-6-4T (1945)												
42269	4MT 2-6-4T (1945)										To Aviemore	X	X
42270	4MT 2-6-4T (1945)												
42271	4MT 2-6-4T (1945)												
42272	4MT 2-6-4T (1945)												
42273	4MT 2-6-4T (1945)												
42695	4MT 2-6-4T (1945)												
54478	3P 4-4-0 (1920)												
54452	3P 4-4-0 (1910)												
69187	3F: N15 0-6-2T (1910)												
64495	3F: J35 0-6-0 (1906)												
64500	3F: J35 0-6-0 (1906)												
64517	3F: J35 0-6-0 (1906)												
64527	3F: J35 0-6-0 (1906)												
56253	3F 0-6-0T (1896)												
56283	3F 0-6-0T (1896)												
56312	3F 0-6-0T (1896)												
56313	3F 0-6-0T (1896)												
57679	3F 0-6-0 (1918)												
57550	3F 0-6-0 (1899)												
57559	3F 0-6-0 (1899)												
57560	3F 0-6-0 (1899)	X	X	X	X	X	X	X	X	X	X	X	Ex Corkerhill
57565	3F 0-6-0 (1899)												
57576	3F 0-6-0 (1899)												
57645	3F 0-6-0 (1899)												
55165	2P 0-4-4T (1900)												
55202	2P 0-4-4T (1900)												
55210	2P 0-4-4T (1900)												
55229	2P 0-4-4T (1900)												
55233	2P 0-4-4T (1900)												
47163	2F 0-6-0T (1928)												

ENGINE ALLOCATION & TRANSFERS : EDINBURGH (DALRY ROAD)

modernisation and until the novelty wore off there was quite a feeling of relief that nationalisation had not put the junior partner in Edinburgh out of the race for capital investment.

It did not take long for the gloss to wear thin. Passengers soon came to realise that the gloom and antiquity of the 0-4-4T's compared favourably with the noise and vibration of the diesels. The operating quickly discovered that the absence of light engine and run-round movements not only led to the loss of jobs but introduced into railway operating a level of dullness that abstracted from the interest of the job.

The worst effected was the motive power department who were no longer to be masters of their charges. Up to the arrival of the units, locomotive matters had been focused on Dalry Road and it had been casually assumed that whatever shape modernisation took, the depot would still be needed to provide and maintain the trains. It came therefore as a considerable shock to discover that not only were new maintenance facilities being built at Leith Central on the North British but that all units required for the Caledonian workings would be provided by the rival system.

Loco	Class	Aug-57	Sep-57	Oct-57	Nov-57	Dec-57	Jan-58	Feb-58	Mar-58	Apr-58	May-58	Jun-58	Jul-58
61246	5MT:B1 4-6-0 (1942)							To E'burgh (SM)	X	X	X	X	X
44994	5MT 4-6-0 (1934)												
45007	5MT 4-6-0 (1934)												To Corkerhill
45022	5MT 4-6-0 (1934)												
45023	5MT 4-6-0 (1934)												
45030	5MT 4-6-0 (1934)												
45036	5MT 4-6-0 (1934)												
45086	5MT 4-6-0 (1934)												
45127	5MT 4-6-0 (1934)												
45155	5MT 4-6-0 (1934)	X	X	X	X	X	X	X	X	Ex Haymarket			
45161	5MT 4-6-0 (1934)												To Corkerhill
45183	5MT 4-6-0 (1934)												
42807	5MT 2-6-0 (1926)												
64536	5F:J37 0-6-0 (1914)												
64554	5F:J37 0-6-0 (1914)												
64561	5F:J37 0-6-0 (1914)												
64574	5F:J37 0-6-0 (1914)												
64591	5F:J37 0-6-0 (1914)												
64612	5F:J37 0-6-0 (1914)												
42268	4MT 2-6-4T (1945)												To Polmadie
42270	4MT 2-6-4T (1945)												
42271	4MT 2-6-4T (1945)												
42272	4MT 2-6-4T (1945)												
42273	4MT 2-6-4T (1945)												
42695	4MT 2-6-4T (1945)												To Polmadie
54478	3P 4-4-0 (1920)												
54452	3P 4-4-0 (1910)	W/D	X	X	X	X	X	X	X	X	X	X	X
69187	3F:N15 0-6-2T (1910)												
64495	3F:J35 0-6-0 (1906)											W/D	X
64500	3F:J35 0-6-0 (1906)												
64517	3F:J35 0-6-0 (1906)												
64527	3F:J35 0-6-0 (1906)												
56253	3F 0-6-0T (1896)												
56283	3F 0-6-0T (1896)												
56312	3F 0-6-0T (1896)												
56313	3F 0-6-0T (1896)												
57679	3F 0-6-0 (1918)												
57550	3F 0-6-0 (1899)												
57559	3F 0-6-0 (1899)												
57560	3F 0-6-0 (1899)												
57565	3F 0-6-0 (1899)												
57576	3F 0-6-0 (1899)												
57645	3F 0-6-0 (1899)												
55165	2P 0-4-4T (1900)												
55202	2P 0-4-4T (1900)												
55210	2P 0-4-4T (1900)												
55229	2P 0-4-4T (1900)												
55233	2P 0-4-4T (1900)												
47163	2F 0-6-0T (1928)												

ENGINE ALLOCATION & TRANSFERS : EDINBURGH (DALRY ROAD)

There was an irony in that the unit which formed the 07.27 Leith North to Princes Street started its day a stones throw away at Leith Central and had to perform an hour and a half's empty running before earning a penny in revenue.

Unfortunately dieselisation did not stop with the Leith services for two months later the Glasgow services went over to multiple-unit operation; the entire service except for one evening rush-hour train in each direction going over to railcars.

The Glasgow railcars operated on the same principle as those on the Leith branch by coming over from Leith Central (NB) each morning and the train service that had traditionally been monopolised by engines from the LMS sheds in Glasgow was henceforth worked by multiple-units from the wrong side of Edinburgh.

As a result of these changes which stripped Princes Street of almost all its operational interest, two Black 5's and a pair of 4MT 2-6-4T's were despatched to Corkerhill and Polmadie respectively whilst most of the 0-4-4T's were taken out of traffic and placed in store.

Steam returned to the Leith line for a week in February 1959 when the railcars had to be temporarily withdrawn for modifications. Relief engines included LMS 2-6-4T's, a V1 2-6-2T, 4-4-0 54478 and a pair of Caledonian 0-6-0's.

Trouble with the multiple units was not confined to those working the Leith branch since a few months after dieselisation, the units on the Princes Street - Glasgow Central workings started to give serious cause for concern.

Hopes that steam would return to the main line did not materialise and instead a number of express multiple units were

ENGINE ALLOCATION & TRANSFERS : EDINBURGH (DALRY ROAD)

Loco	Class	Aug-58	Sep-58	Oct-58	Nov-58	Dec-58	Jan-59	Feb-59	Mar-59	Apr-59	May-59	Jun-59	Jul-59
44994	5MT 4-6-0 (1934)												
45022	5MT 4-6-0 (1934)												
45023	5MT 4-6-0 (1934)												
45030	5MT 4-6-0 (1934)												
45036	5MT 4-6-0 (1934)												
45086	5MT 4-6-0 (1934)												
45127	5MT 4-6-0 (1934)												
45155	5MT 4-6-0 (1934)												
45183	5MT 4-6-0 (1934)												
42807	5MT 2-6-0 (1926)												
64794	5F: J39 0-6-0 (1926)	X	Ex E'burgh (SM)										
64946	5F: J39 0-6-0 (1926)	X	Ex E'burgh (SM)										
64963	5F: J39 0-6-0 (1926)	X	Ex E'burgh (SM)										
64986	5F: J39 0-6-0 (1926)	X	Ex E'burgh (SM)										
64536	5F: J37 0-6-0 (1914)		To E'burgh (SM)	X	X	X	X	X	X	X	X	X	X
64554	5F: J37 0-6-0 (1914)												
64561	5F: J37 0-6-0 (1914)												
64569	5F: J37 0-6-0 (1914)	X	X	X	X	X	X	X	Ex Stirling				
64574	5F: J37 0-6-0 (1914)		To E'burgh (SM)	X	X	X	X	X	X	X	X	X	X
64591	5F: J37 0-6-0 (1914)		To E'burgh (SM)	X	X	X	X	X	X	X	X	X	X
64612	5F: J37 0-6-0 (1914)		To E'burgh (SM)	X	X	X	X	X	X	X	X	X	X
42270	4MT 2-6-4T (1945)												To Corkerhill
42271	4MT 2-6-4T (1945)						To Perth	X	X	X	X	X	X
42272	4MT 2-6-4T (1945)												
42273	4MT 2-6-4T (1945)												
67668	3P: V1 2-6-2T (1930)	X	X	X	X	X	X	X	X	X	X	X	Ex E'burgh (SM)
54478	3P 4-4-0 (1920)												
69187	3F: N15 0-6-2T (1910)												
64497	3F: J35 0-6-0 (1906)	X	X	X	X	X	X	X	Ex Stirling				
64500	3F: J35 0-6-0 (1906)												
64501	3F: J35 0-6-0 (1906)	X	X	X	X	X	X	X	Ex Stirling				
64517	3F: J35 0-6-0 (1906)		W/D	X	X	X	X	X	X	X	X	X	X
64527	3F: J35 0-6-0 (1906)												
56253	3F 0-6-0T (1896)					W/D	X	X	X	X	X	X	X
56283	3F 0-6-0T (1896)	W/D	X	X	X	X	X	X	X	X	X	X	X
56312	3F 0-6-0T (1896)												
56313	3F 0-6-0T (1896)												
57679	3F 0-6-0 (1918)									To Stirling	X	X	X
57550	3F 0-6-0 (1899)												
57559	3F 0-6-0 (1899)												
57560	3F 0-6-0 (1899)												
57565	3F 0-6-0 (1899)												
57576	3F 0-6-0 (1899)									To Stirling	X	X	X
57645	3F 0-6-0 (1899)												
55165	2P 0-4-4T (1900)				To Haymarket	X	X	X	X	X	X	Ex Haymarket	
55202	2P 0-4-4T (1900)												
55210	2P 0-4-4T (1900)												
55229	2P 0-4-4T (1900)												
55233	2P 0-4-4T (1900)												
47163	2F 0-6-0T (1928)												
D3736	0F: Diesel 0-6-0	X	X	X	X	X	X	X	X	X	NEW		
D3737	0F: Diesel 0-6-0	X	X	X	X	X	X	X	X	X	NEW		
D3738	0F: Diesel 0-6-0	X	X	X	X	X	X	X	X	X	X	NEW	
D3739	0F: Diesel 0-6-0	X	X	X	X	X	X	X	X	X	NEW		
D3740	0F: Diesel 0-6-0	X	X	X	X	X	X	X	X	X	NEW	To E'burgh (SM)	X
D3741	0F: Diesel 0-6-0	X	X	X	X	X	X	X	X	X	X	NEW	
D3742	0F: Diesel 0-6-0	X	X	X	X	X	X	X	X	X	X	NEW	

obtained from the Western Region in order to keep the service going. What with GWR Pannier tanks being transferred from Croes Newydd and Bristol to Helmsdale to work the Dornoch branch, the world was becoming smaller.

Goods traffic continued to be steam hauled but even in this arena, changes were made as the aging J37's were replaced by LNER standard J39 0-6-0's. Yard shunting, however, did not remain steam worked since the summer of 1959 saw an influx of 0-6-0 diesel shunters - later replaced by 0-4-0 engines which were found to be better suited to dock work.

Having absorbed so many LNER engines since 1948, in December 1959 Dalry Road made a gesture of repayment by sending 0-4-4T 55165 to Haymarket for pilot work at Edinburgh Waverley. The state of the engine was such that it was deemed unusable and after six months languishing at the back of Haymarket MPD - during which time its work was covered by a diesel shunter - it returned to Dalry Road.

The early 1960's saw many of the Dalry Road allocation being withdrawn for scrap yet in spite of its passenger services being based at Leith Central, the shed managed to survive until 1965, its allocation for the last few years consisting of no more than a handful of Black 5's and B1's for working goods traffic between Leith and Glasgow.

| | | | | | | | | ENGINE ALLOCATION & TRANSFERS : EDINBURGH (DALRY ROAD) | | | | | |
Loco	Class	Aug-59	Sep-59	Oct-59	Nov-59	Dec-59	Jan-60	Feb-60	Mar-60	Apr-60	May-60	Jun-60	Jul-60
61007	5MT: B1 4-6-0 (1942)	X	X	X	X	X	X	X	X	X	X	X	Ex Haymarket
61244	5MT: B1 4-6-0 (1942)	X	X	X	X	X	X	X	X	X	X	X	Ex Haymarket
61260	5MT: B1 4-6-0 (1942)	X	X	X	X	X	X	X	X	X	X	Ex E'burgh (SM)	
44994	5MT 4-6-0 (1934)												
45022	5MT 4-6-0 (1934)												
45023	5MT 4-6-0 (1934)												
45030	5MT 4-6-0 (1934)												
45036	5MT 4-6-0 (1934)												
45086	5MT 4-6-0 (1934)												
45127	5MT 4-6-0 (1934)												
45155	5MT 4-6-0 (1934)												
45183	5MT 4-6-0 (1934)												
42807	5MT 2-6-0 (1926)												
64794	5F: J39 0-6-0 (1926)												
64946	5F: J39 0-6-0 (1926)												
64963	5F: J39 0-6-0 (1926)												To Dunfermline
64986	5F: J39 0-6-0 (1926)												
64554	5F: J37 0-6-0 (1914)												
64561	5F: J37 0-6-0 (1914)												
64569	5F: J37 0-6-0 (1914)												
80086	4MT 2-6-4T (1951)	X	X	X	X	X	X	X	X	X	Ex Chester		
42272	4MT 2-6-4T (1945)												
42273	4MT 2-6-4T (1945)												
67668	3P: V1 2-6-2T (1930)												
54478	3P 4-4-0 (1920)												
69187	3F: N15 0-6-2T (1910)					W/D	X	X	X	X	X	X	X
64497	3F: J35 0-6-0 (1906)												
64500	3F: J35 0-6-0 (1906)												
64501	3F: J35 0-6-0 (1906)	W/D	X	X	X	X	X	X	X	X	X	X	X
64527	3F: J35 0-6-0 (1906)												
56312	3F 0-6-0T (1896)												
56313	3F 0-6-0T (1896)												
57550	3F 0-6-0 (1899)												
57559	3F 0-6-0 (1899)												
57560	3F 0-6-0 (1899)												
57565	3F 0-6-0 (1899)												
57645	3F 0-6-0 (1899)												
55165	2P 0-4-4T (1900)												
55202	2P 0-4-4T (1900)												
55210	2P 0-4-4T (1900)												
55229	2P 0-4-4T (1900)												
55233	2P 0-4-4T (1900)												
47163	2F 0-6-0T (1928)												
D3560	0F: Diesel 0-6-0	X	X	X	X	X	X	X	Ex Haymarket				
D3561	0F: Diesel 0-6-0	X	X	X	X	X	X	X	X	NEW			
D3736	0F: Diesel 0-6-0												To E'burgh (SM)
D3737	0F: Diesel 0-6-0												
D3738	0F: Diesel 0-6-0								To Haymarket	X	X	X	X
D3739	0F: Diesel 0-6-0								To Haymarket	X	X	X	X
D3741	0F: Diesel 0-6-0												To E'burgh (SM)
D3742	0F: Diesel 0-6-0		To E'burgh (SM)	X	X	X	X	X	X	X	X	X	X
D3877	0F: Diesel 0-6-0	X	X	X	X	X	X	X	X	X	X	X	Ex E'burgh (SM)
D2745	0F: 0-4-0 Diesel	X	X	X	X	X	X	X	X	X	Ex E'burgh (SM)		
D2754	0F: 0-4-0 Diesel	X	X	X	X	X	X	X	X	X	Ex Grangmth		
D2755	0F: 0-4-0 Diesel	X	X	X	X	X	X	X	X	X	NEW		

The 08.40 Glasgow Central to Edinburgh express and the 11.37 stopping train back to Glasgow were booked to a class 5 4-6-0 but often produced a larger engine, rangng from a 5XP Jubilee to a Coronation Pacific.

A batch of new 6MT Clan Class Pacifics arrived at Polmadie to take over the through workings to Manchester Victoria from the 5XP 4-6-0's which had been giving trouble but it was not long before the new Pacifics were found to be worse than the engines they had been built to replace and although they remained on the Manchester duties throughout the 1950's, they were often seen on lesser duties such as those between Glasgow and Edinburgh.

On 23rd February 1952 Clan 4-6-2 72003 'Clan Fraser' stands at the head of the 11.37 Princes Street to Glasgow Central.   Across the platform Perth-based Black Five 4-6-0 44796 waits to follow with the 11.40 Edinburgh to Perth.

None too conscious of the edicts regarding the emission of smoke, the fireman of Clan Pacific 72003 'Clan Fraser' gets his engine hot for the 13.30 express to Glasgow Central.   The dilemma lay in the fact that use of the blower would clear the smoke away but would burn through the coal too quickly.   The alternative was to fill the firebox and hope that the coal was relatively smokeless.   Although warranting open lights, in reality there was little to distinguish the 13.30 from many of the stopping trains since it called at almost every station between Slateford and Bellshill.   In the eyes of the timing clerk, the fact it ran non-stop over the eleven miles from Bellshill to Glasgow made the difference between a stopping train and an express.

...........and a few minutes later the smoke clears without the blower being needed.. All that is needed now is some steam; something which cannot be taken for granted on a Clan

72003

One of the Carlisle Clans, 72005 'Clan MacGregor' shuts off steam at Merchiston and prepares for the Slateford stop with the 13.30 Princes Street to Glasgow Central on 23rd May 1954. By the time of the photograph very few illusions remained about the Clans and even though the load was a mere six coaches, the 20-mile climb from Slateford to Benhar would almost certainly be a challenge for the fireman if not the engine.

Very soon after entering service, Clan 6MT 72003 accelerates an Edinburgh - Glasgow express past Dalry Road shed. Even in BR days the Caledonian practice of displaying route indicators remained mandatory for all trains except Anglo-Scottish services in the ex-CR Edinburgh and Glasgow districts. In reality however there was always a shortage of indicators and engines were as likely to enter service without them as with. The route displayed on 72003 is that for Edinburgh to Glasgow and vice versa.

what the timetable stated, the two coaches went through to Euston and returned in a rather roundabout way by working to Glasgow in the Midday Scot and the 09.50 Glasgow - Edinburgh the following day.

Taking eleven and a half hours to reach London, the 17.35 was probably the most miserable service operated by the West Coast - and that is saying a great deal - but the historical connection was appreciated by enthusiasts as was the fact that the Glasgow and Edinburgh sections combined, not at Carstairs but at Symington, seven miles further along the main line towards Carlisle. The great thing about combing two sections at Symington was that the Edinburgh portion did not change direction as was the case when the operation was done at Carstairs and one did not therefore have to move to find another window seat facing the engine.

The idea of two major expresses coming to a halt and joining together at the generally unremarkable station of Symington, population 650, seemed something of an anachronism by the 1950's and its operational survival was due to the cramped facilities at Carstairs where coupling up Edinburgh and Glasgow sections into one train blocked not only the up and down platforms but most of the running lines as well. In many cases it was easier to run the Edinburgh portion into the bay platform at Symington, run the engine round the train and shunt it onto the rear of the Glasgow express when it arrived in the up main platform.

Occasionally combinations had to be booked for Carstairs, one such being the afternoon Manchester service which, had it merged with the Glasgow coaches at Symington, would have done so at the same time as the 11.15 Birmingham - Glasgow was shedding its Princes Street coaches. This, the authorities deemed, would have strained the resources of such a small location and since Carstairs was relatively quiet at that time of day, the general rule was waived.

The fact that the Edinburgh portions appeared to be poor relatives of the Glasgow sections, did not mean they were necessarily devoid of interest. During the late 1940's the afternoon Lancashire departure from Princes Street conveyed through coaches for the 15.55 Glasgow Central to Liverpool (Exchange) and the 16.12 Glasgow to Manchester (Victoria). There were three vehicles in each section and it does not need a great deal of imagination to picture the fireworks that such a relatively heavy load could induce from its Compound 4-4-0 as it made its way up to Cobbinshaw Summit.

The operation was more complicated than usual and the melding of trains was therefore performed at Carstairs although, to let the earlier train get ahead, the Manchester service was given a two-minute call at Symington.

Curiously, both sets of coaches returned from Liverpool, the Manchester vehicles being used for the 06.05 Manchester Victoria to Liverpool before forming the 14.15 back to Edinburgh whilst the other set returned to Princes Street in the 16.30 from Liverpool.

In 1950 the both Manchester and Liverpool services were merged into one service from Glasgow with the Edinburgh portion being reduced to three coaches for Manchester Victoria.

Given that Birmingham ranked equal in size and importance with Manchester and Liverpool yet was virtually inaccessible from Edinburgh Waverley, it was surprising that Princes Street was only given one through day service to New Street. What, however, the service lacked in frequency it made up for in other ways by - south of Symington - being the only regular up service on the Caledonian to be worked by a Camden Coronation Pacific. The working was also notable because its fourteen vehicles included three articulated twins, one of which formed part of the four-coach Edinburgh portion. Articulation was rare in any degree on the London Midland and three examples in one train was an exceptional sight.

Apart from a handful of trains to Kingsknowe on

Cont. Page 36

EDINBURGH, GRANTON, HAYMARKET & LEITH

Train	21.35			21.25	04.30		03.30	02.25	02.25	04.20	05.10	06.30		07.15	07.15		06.33			06.40		05.45	08.26
From	Dumfries			&St	D'zell		M'end	K'moor	K'moor	M'end	B'ton	Shotts		C'strs	C'strs		G'gow			S.Jcn		C'lisle	Lanark
Class	C	K	C	E	F	TPO	H	D	D	H	F	B	K	K	K	ECS	B	B	B	B	F	E	B
CARSTAIRS			03.36			04.46							07.09	07.15						07.59			08.40
Dolphintown Jn								05.10							07.15							08/11	
Carnwath													07.14	07.23	07.30					08.04			
Auchengray													07.22	07.45	07.52					08.12			
Wilsontown Jcn																							
Cobbinshaw			03.49			04.59		05.32					07.29		(To					08.19		08.35	08.53
Harburn								05.37					07.34		W'ton					08.24		08.40	
Midcalder Jcn	01/09		03.57	04.10	04.30	05.07	05.17	05.43		06.50	07.03	07.20	07.39	Colly)				08.07		08.29	08.48	08.49	09.01
Midcalder												07.23						08.10		08.32			
Camps Jcn																							
Ravelrig Jcn																					08.58		
Kingsknowe												07.33						08.20	08.34	08.42		08.57	
Slateford												07.36		07.55				08.23	08.37	08.45		09.00	
Balerno Jcn																							09.12
Slateford Yard		01.30					05.38	06.00	06.30	07.10	07.25											09.02	
Merchiston	01/21		04.06	04.25	04.46	05.16						07.39	07.50	08.00			08.02	08.26	08.40	08.48		09.03	09.15
Morrison St Gds					(To																		
Lothian Road Gds		01.35			Crew						06.40												
PRINCES STREET	01.29		04.10		Jn)	05.19						07.43	07.54				08.06	08.30	08.44	08.52		09.07	09.19

Train					01.40	02.23	04.35						07.15				08.40				09.05		10.00		
From					Crew Jn	Crew Jn	Crew Jn						S'frd				Crew Jn				S'frd		Crew Jn		
Class	E	H	H	K	J	J	J	ECS	K	B	B	K	K	B	A	ECS	J	K	B	K	A	J	A	K	B
PRINCES STREET								05.50		06.27	06.47			08.02	08.38	08.42			09.25		10.10		10.50		11.37
Lothian Road Gds				01.10					05.55																
Morrison St Gds																									
Merchiston	00.01	00.23	00.50							06.31	06.51			08.06	08.42	08.45			09.29		10.13		10.53		11.41
Slateford Yard				01.15					06.05				07.15							09.05		10.55			
Balerno Jcn																						11.00			
Slateford					01.55	02.38	04.50							08.09		08.58							10.18		11.44
Kingsknowe																		08.49							11.47
Ravelrig Jcn																			09.31	09.41					
Camps Jcn																									
Midcalder										06.46	07.05	07.50	08.00	08.23	08.56				09.43						11.59
Midcalder Jcn	00/34	01/01	01/28		02/34	03/17	05/29		06/12	06/49	07/08	07.50	08/05	08/26	08/59			09/36	09/46	09/56	10/26		10/57	11/07	12/02
Harburn											07.16								09.54						
Cobbinshaw	00/56	01/35																	10.01		10/36		11/17		
Wilsontown Jcn																									
Auchengray											07.27								10.07						
Carnwath											07.34								10.14						
Dolphintown Jn	01/11	01/56																			10/48		11/29		
CARSTAIRS		02.00									07.38								10.18						
Dest	K'moor		Moss'd		Clyde	Clyde	Clyde	Shotts		G'gow			W'muir	G'gow	G'gow	S'stone			Lanark	B'har	B'ham	D'zll	L'pool		G'gow

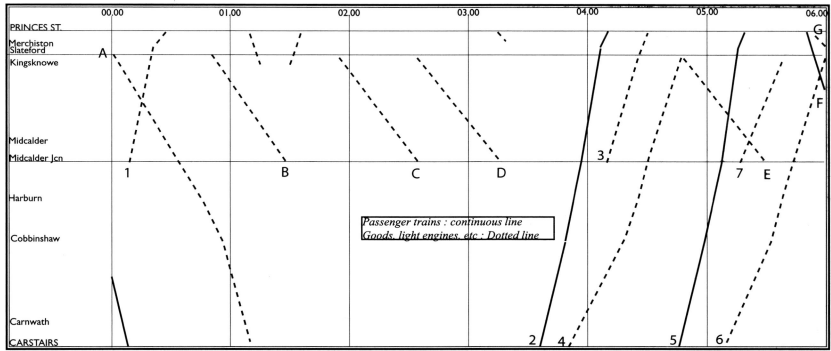

| | 00.00 | 01.00 | 02.00 | 03.00 | 04.00 | 05.00 | 06.00 |

PRINCES ST.

Merchiston
Slateford

Kingsknowe

Midcalder
Midcalder Jcn

Harburn

Cobbinshaw

Carnwath

CARSTAIRS

Passenger trains : continuous line
Goods, light engines, etc : Dotted line

TRAFFIC MOVEMENTS. *Unlike most main lines the Eastern section of the Caledonian was rather quiet during the night. Passenger and mineral traffic was absent leaving only a pair of goods trains from Slateford yard and the iron ore traffic from Leith Docks which was marshalled and worked from Crew Junction, Granton. Leading the pack is the 00.01 Slateford to Carlisle Kingmoor class E express goods, a 5MT 2-6-0 turn which returns with the 05.45 Carlisle (Viaduct) to Edinburgh (Lothian Road). Passing it in the vicinity of Ravelrig is the 21.35 Dumfries - Princes Street Milk; a circuitous working which takes a 5MT 2-6-0 to Dumfries via the Caledonian main line and Lockerbie, returning via the GSWR route.*

Following the 00.01 Slateford to Carlisle - albeit by a handsome margin - is the 00.50 Slateford to Mossend class H, a J37 duty which clears Edinburgh of any traffic it has for Scotland other than Glasgow.

Ref	Train	From	Dest
A	00.01	Slateford	Kingmoor
B	00.50	Slateford	Mossend
C	01.40	Crew Jcn	Rutherglen
D	02.23	Crew Jcn	Newton
E	04.35	Crew Jcn	Rutherglen
F	06.47	Princes St	Shotts (ECS)
I	21.35	Dumfries	Princes St
2	23.20	**Manchester**	**Princes St**
3	02.15	Buchanan St	Lothian Rd
4	02.55	Dalzell	Crew Jcn
5	20.30	**Euston**	**Princes St**
6	03.30	Mossend	Slateford
7	02.25	Kingmoor	Lothian Rd

Mossend is located in the maelstrom of lines where the Carlisle - Aberdeen and Edinburgh - Glasgow routes bisect each other and is probably the most important of the marshalling yards on the system. The remainder of the up goods service is comprised of two iron-ore trains for Carmyle (Clyde Iron Works) and one for Clyde's Mill works at Newton.

The shift sees almost nothing on the down road until almost four o'clock when the first of the overnight services enters the district. This is the Edinburgh section of the 23.20 Manchester Exchange parcels and its running is watched very closely since it is booked to be followed by the 02.55 Dalzell - Crew Junction empties, the latter running on a fairly tight margin ahead of the 20.30 Euston - Edinburgh T.P.O and the 02.25 Kingmoor - Edinburgh express goods.

EDINBURGH - CARSTAIRS WORKING TIMETABLE (PASSENGER & GOODS) : 1955

Train	06.40	05.45	07.15	08.40	08.15	09.50		10.45	10.20	10.45	10.00	10.00	10.45		10.45		12.19		13.15		10.00	09.30		11.30	11.30
From	S. Jcn	C'lisle	C. Mill	G'gow	G'gow	G'gow		C'strs	M'kirk	C'strs	Clyde	W. Jcn	C'strs		C'strs		G'gow		C'strs		W. Jcn	M'ter		Benhar	Benhar
Class	F	E	F	A	B	A	K	K	B	K	F	K	K	B	K	B	B	J	J	B	K	A	K	K	K
CARSTAIRS							10.45		11.36													14.48			
Dolphintown Jn																			13.15						
Carnwath							11.00	11.20	11.41																
Auchengray							11.35		11.50	12.00									13.33		13.40				
Wilsontown Jcn																			13/47						
Cobbinshaw									11.57	12.15		12.35							(To Colly)			15/01			
Harburn									12.03				13.05		13.15										
Midcalder Jcn			09/12	09/41	10/06	10/55			12/08		12/13	12/57	13/23		13/38							15/09		15.12	
Midcalder					10.09				12.11			13.00			13.41							15.17			
Camps Jcn													13.30											15.22	15.27
Ravelrig Jcn	09.08																								(To Camps)
Kingsknowe					10.19							13.06		13.41		13.51				14.03					
Slateford	09/21		09/30		10.22				12.22		12/30	13.09		13.44		13.54				14.06					
Balerno Jcn	(To		(To								(To														
Slateford Yard	Crew	09.30	Crew																		14.15			15.50	
Merchiston	Jn)		Jn)	09/50	10.25	11/04			12.25		Jn)	13.12		13.47		13.57				14.09		15.20			
Morrison St Gds																							16.00		
Lothian Road Gds		09.40																							
PRINCES STREET				09.53	10.29	11.07			12.29			13.16		13.51		14.01				14.13		15.24			

Train								13.35																	
From								Crew Jn																	
Class	B	K	B	K	B	B	A	K	J	K	K	B	B	A	K	K	A	A	Milk	K	B	B	B	B	B
PRINCES STREET	12.06		12.32		13.04	13.18	13.30					15.20	15.45	16.05			16.40	16.48			17.15	17.35	17.38	17.55	18.12
Lothian Road Gds										15.05	15.10									17/00					
Morrison St Gds		12.20																	17.05						
Merchiston	12.10		12.36		13.08	13/21	13/33					15/23	15.49	16/08			16/43	16/51	17/08		17.19	17/38	17.42	17.59	18.16
Slateford Yard		12/30						15.10	15.20											17.05					
Balerno Jcn																									
Slateford	12.13		12.39		13.11		13.35		14/01				15.52								17.23		17.45	18.02	18.19
Kingsknowe	12.15		12.41		13.13								15.55								17.26		17/47	18.05	18.22
Ravelrig Jcn							(Ex Camps)																		
Camps Jcn																									
Midcalder						13.35						15.37	16.07					17.05				17.38	17.52	18.17	18.34
Midcalder Jcn						13/38	13/49	13/58	14/42			15/40	16/10	16/22		16/57		17/08	17/29			17/41	17/55	18/20	18/37
Harburn						13.46						15.48	16.16										18.03	18.28	
Cobbinshaw						13.53	14/12					15.55	16/32						17/40					18.10	
Wilsontown Jcn				13/10	13/19											16/50									
Auchengray						13.59						16.01				16/55	17.00							18.16	18.40
Carnwath						14.06												17.35						18.23	
Dolphintown Jn							14.30									17/20			17.58					18/27	
CARSTAIRS					13.37	14.10						16.10	16.45			17/23		17.39						18.50	
Dest						Lanark	G'gow		S'stn			Lanark	G'gow	M'ter		Law Jn	G'gow	Muir'k	Dum'fs		G'gow	Euston		Lanark	G'gow

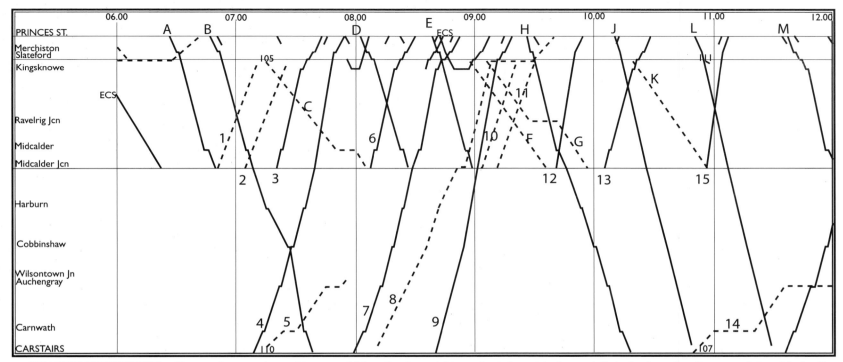

PRINCES ST.	A B D E ECS H J L M	
Merchiston		
Slateford	105	
Kingsknowe	K	
ECS	C	
Ravelrig Jcn		
Midcalder	1 6 10 F G	
Midcalder Jcn	2 3 12 13 15	
Harburn		
Cobbinshaw		
Wilsontown Jn		
Auchengray		
Carnwath	4 5 7 8 9 14	
CARSTAIRS	110 107	

TRAFFIC MOVEMENTS. *Not even its staunchest advocate could describe the Carstairs line as being busy but when its traffic is merged with that of the Glasgow route, the result is an interesting mix of services east of Midcalder which even includes a rush-hour of sorts into Edinburgh. One thing that has to be watched carefully is the running of the goods trains due to pass Midcalder Junction around 07.00. These - the 04.20 Mossend and the 05.10 Bridgeton - have rather tight paths ahead of the first Glasgow and Carstairs passengers and have the potential to cause trouble. Should there be a problem one can be berthed at Ravelrig whilst the other can use the up loop on the Glasgow line at Midcalder Junction.*

Even if the Mossend and Bridgeton freights scrape into Slateford without knocking anything, one's guard cannot be allowed to drop since there are a number of

Ref	Train	From	Dest	Ref	Train	From	Dest
A	**06.27**	**Princes St**	**Glasgow**	2	05.10	Bridgeton	Slateford
B	**06.47**	**Princes St**	**Carstairs**	3	**06.50**	**Shotts**	**Prines St**
C	07.15	Slateford	Woodmuir Jcn	4	**07.09**	**Carstairs**	**Princes St**
D	**08.02**	**Princes St**	**Glasgow**	5	07.15	Carstairs	Kingshill
E	**08.38**	**Princes St**	**Glasgow**	6	**06.35**	**Glasgow**	**Princes St**
F	08.40	Crew Jcn	Shettleston	7	**07.59**	**Carstairs**	**Princes St**
G	09.05	Slateford	Benhar Jcn	8	05.45	Carlisle	Lothian Rd
H	**09.25**	**Princes St**	**Lanark**	9	08.26	Lanark	Princes St
J	**10.10**	**Princes St**	**Birmingham**	10	06.40	Strathclyde	Crew Jn
K	10.00	Crew Jcn	Dalzell	11	07.15	Newton	Crew Jn
L	**10.50**	**Princes St**	**Manchester**	12	**08.40**	**Glasgow**	**Princes St**
M	**11.37**	**Princes St**	**Glasgow**	13	**08.15**	**Glasgow**	**Princes St**
I	04.20	Mossend	Slateford	14	10.45	Carstairs	Camps Jcn
				15	**09.50**	**Glasgow**	**Princes St**

tight margins to be watched, especially in the down direction around nine o'clock. One particularly unforgivable clash occurs at Midcalder Junction; the 06.40 Strathclyde to Crew Junction being booked - thanks to an amazing piece of optimism on the part of the timing clerk - to pass at the same time as the 05.45 Carlisle (Viaduct) to Edinburgh. In practice the Strathclyde has to be looped at Midcalder Junction until the Carlisle goods and the 08.26 Lanark passenger have cleared the section.

Probably the most interesting trains of the morning are the 10.10 and 10.50 departures from Princes Street which run not to Carstairs but up the Caledonian main line to Symington where they attach to the 10.05 Glasgow - Birmingham and the 10.40 Glasgow - Manchester respectively. Four coaches are worked from Edinburgh for each service and the Birmingham working is of especial interest since it contains one of the LMS articulated twin sets.

EDINBURGH - CARSTAIRS WORKING TIMETABLE (PASSENGER & GOODS) : 1955

Train		14.08	11.30	15.00	16.15	15.42		16.30	17.16		17.15			18.00		18.50		19.33	19.10		18.00		21.25	
From		S'ton	Benhar	Dal'l	Lanark	G'gow		G'gow	Sym		G'gow			G'gow		G'gow		Cstrs	S'ton		C'lisle		G'gow	
Class	A	F	K	F	B	B	K	A	A	B	B	K	B	B	H	B	K	H	F	A	E	A	B	E
CARSTAIRS	15.30			15.50	16.30					17.46			18.50		19.33					21.00		21.30		
Dolphintown Jn									17/25						19/40						21/04			
Carnwath					16.35					17.51			18.55											
Auchengray					16.43					17.59			19.03											
Wilsontown Jcn																								
Cobbinshaw	15/43			16/18	16.50				17/37	18/04			19.10		20.06			20.21		21/13	21/27	21/43		
Harburn				16/24	16.55								19.15					20/30			21/32			
Midcalder Jcn	15/51	16/05	(Ex	16/32	17/00	17/10		17/33	17/45	18/13	18/26		19/20	19/26		20/02		20/38	21/06	21/21	21/39	21/52	22/41	
Midcalder			Camps)		17.03	17.13				18.16			19.23	19.29		20.05							22.44	
Camps Jcn			16.15																					
Ravelrig Jcn																								
Kingsknowe										18.26														
Slateford						17.24																		
Balerno Jcn																								
Slateford Yard		16/22	16.35	16/55			17.30					19.02					20.30	20.55	21/23		21.55			23.00
Merchiston	16.02				17.15	17.27		17.44	17/57	18.30	18.47		19.35	19.41		20.17				21/30		22/02	22/54	
Morrison St Gds		(To		(To															(To					
Lothian Road Gds		Crew		Crew			17.40					19.20					20.35		Crew					23.10
PRINCES STREET	16.06	Jn)		Jn)	17.19	17.31		17.48	18.00	18.34	18.51		19.39	19.45		20.21			Jn)	21.33		22.05	22.57	

Train									21.55				23.00
From									Crew Jn				Crew Jn
Class	TPO	K	A	C	K	A	B	E	A	J	F	A	H	H
PRINCES STREET	18.38		19.30		20.00	21.05	21.28		22.05			23.30		
Lothian Road Gds		18.42												
Morrison St Gds														
Merchiston	18/41		19/33			21/08	21/31		22/08			23/33		
Slateford Yard		18.47		20.00	20.07			21.38		22/12	22.55		23.40	23.15
Balerno Jcn														
Slateford														
Kingsknowe														
Ravelrig Jcn														
Camps Jcn														
Midcalder			19.47				21.45		22.22					
Midcalder Jcn	18/54		19/50	20/25		21/21	21/48	22/10	22/25	22/51	23/28	23/47	00/18	
Harburn				20/38					22.33					
Cobbinshaw	19/04			20/47		21/31			22.40			23/47		
Wilsontown Jcn														
Auchengray														
Carnwath									22.51					
Dolphintown Jn				21/00										
CARSTAIRS	19.15					21.42			22.55			00.08		
Dest			G'gow	K'moor			G'gow	B. St		D'zll	M'end		Pol'd	

Thanks for assistance with text and illustrations are due to Glen Woods, D. Randles, J. Lewis, P. Davey, S. Thompson, W. Ware, M. Bentley, P, Webb, W. Becket, Alan Cliff, J. Cat, Jeremy Suter, Roger Bell, Harry Townley and Len Hobday.

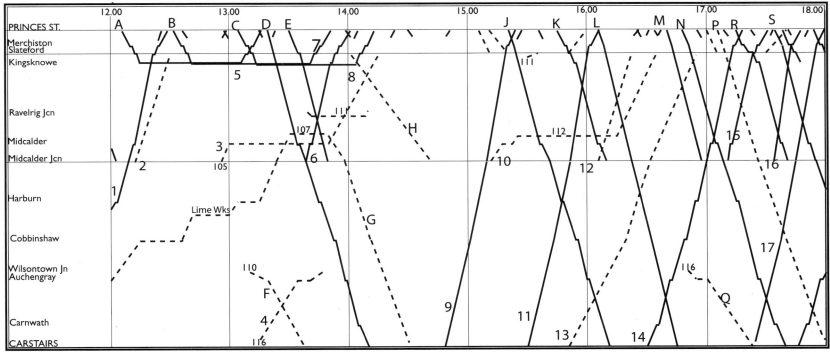

TRAFFIC MOVEMENTS. *A noticeable lull in passenger movements falls on the line after the departure of the 11.37 Edinburgh to Glasgow and apart from a little 0-4-4T activity to and from Kingsknowe, passengers trains become the exception until tea time. The pause allows goods traffic to flow more easily, especially Target 107 and its Carstairs 0-6-0 which serves intermediate stations between Carstairs and Camps. 107 is a trip shared between the Edinburgh and Glasgow roads and makes an earlier run Symington prior to leaving Carstairs for Camps. On Tuesdays and Thursdays it does not appear north of Carstairs at all and operates instead between Carstairs and Elvanfoot, near Beattock.*

The Balerno branch - a sharply graded line which runs parallel to the main line between Balerno and

Ref	Train	From	Dest	Ref	Train	From	Dest
A	12.06	Princes St	Kingsknowe	I	10.20	Muirkirk	Princes St
B	12.32	Princes St	Kingsknowe	2	10.00	Rutherglen	Crew Jcn
C	13.04	Princes St	Kingsknowe	3	10.00	Woodmuir Jn	Slateford
D	13.18	Princes St	Lanark	4	13.15	Carstairs	Kingshill
E	13.30	Princes St	Glasgow	5	13.06	Kingknowe	Princes St
F	12.35	Kingshill	Carstairs	6	12.19	Glasgow	Princes St
G	13.50	Camps	Carstairs	7	13.41	Kingknowe	Princes St
H	13.35	Crew Jcn	Shettleston	8	14.03	Kingknowe	Princes St
J	15.20	Princes St	Lanark	9	09.30	Manchester	Princes St
K	15.45	Princes St	Glasgow	10	11.50	Benhar Jcn	Slateford
L	16.05	Princes St	Manchester	11	15.30	Carstairs	Princes St
M	16.40	Princes St	Glasgow	12	14.08	Shettleston	Crew Jcn
N	16.48	Princes St	Muirkirk	13	15.00	Dalzell	Crew Jcn
P	17.05	Morrison St	Dumfries	14	16.15	Lanark	Princes St
Q	16.10	Wilsontown	Law Jcn	15	15.42	Glasgow	Princes St
R	17.15	Princes St	Glasgow	16	16.30	Glasgow	Princes St
S	17.35	Princes St	Euston	17	11.15	Birmingham	Princes St

Ravelrig Junctions - disappeared from public view in November 1943 when it lost its (very frequent) passenger service and the only remaining movement over the line is Target 111 which submerges around 14.00 at Ravelrig Junction before retracing its steps down the branch to Slateford. A good proportion of its traffic comes from the quarries in the vicinity of Balerno.

Freight activity at the Carstairs end of the line is maintained by Targets 110 and 116 which serve Kingshill, Climpy and Wilsontown collieries, the output of which is used in the Glasgow steel industry. Target 110 finishes its day at Carstairs but Target 116 on its final trip takes a through load of coal from Wilsontown to Law Junction. Both trains are worked by Caledonian 3F 0-6-0's.

Towards the end of the period, passenger traffic from Edinburgh becomes quite intense.

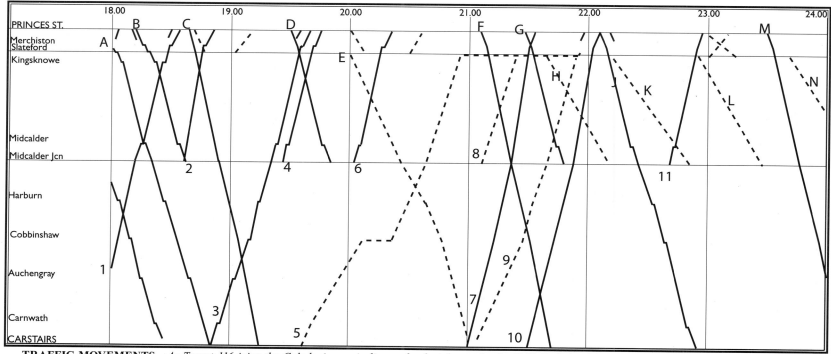

TRAFFIC MOVEMENTS. *As Target 116 joins the Caledonian main line and heads towards Law Junction and, at the other end of the line, Target 112 pulls into Slateford from Benhar, local goods workings come to an end for the day. This early cessation allows Slateford Yard time to shunt out the trips and assemble the night express services which leave at 20.00 for Carlisle Kingmoor (Fully fitted), 21.38 to Glasgow (Buchanan Street), 22.55 to Mossend and 23.40 to Glasgow (Polmadie).*

The remaining main line goods services are the 'whippers-in', clearing the last of the day's traffic from Carstairs and Carlisle respectively. The Carstairs service is quite an interesting working since it involves a Carstairs engine (a Black 5 4-6-0) and men working through to Crew Junction on the Leith branch and returning with the 23.00 to Carstairs. Two stops are made on the down leg of the diagram; one at Cobbinshaw to detach cattle and the other at Slateford to remove the Edinburgh section which is left to

be taken up by the 18.00 Carlisle - Morrison Street.

The latter follows the 21.00 Carstairs - Princes Street express - the Edinburgh connection with the down Midday Scot - and its Kingmoor 2-6-0 has to run hard in order to keep ahead of the afternoon Liverpool - Edinburgh express: the margin between the two trains becoming uncomfortably narrow the far side of Midcalder.

On the passenger front the main item of interest is the 23.30 departure from Princes Street which is a through service to Birmingham, arriving at 06.50. In contrast to pre-war days, there are no sleeping cars for London and the Black 5 with its three carriages for New Street is indistinguishable from the local trains of the area. One must be grateful that a semblance of through traffic remains although there is an irony in that the only LMS services to London depart from the Waverley. These, of course, are the Midland expresses to St Pancras.

Ref	Train	From	Dest	Ref	Train	From	Dest
A	17.55	Princes St	Lanark	I	17.46	Carstairs	Princes St
B	18.12	Princes St	Glasgow	2	16.30	Glasgow	Princes St
C	18.38	Princes St	Carstairs	3	18.50	Carstairs	Princes St
D	19.30	Princes St	Glasgow	4	18.00	Glasgow	Princes St
E	20.00	Slateford	Kingmoor	5	19.33	Carstairs	Crew Jcn
F	21.05	Princes St	Carstairs	6	18.50	Glasgow	Princes St
G	21.28	Princes St	Glasgow	7	21.00	Carstairs	Princes St
H	21.38	Slateford	Buchanan St	8	19.10	Shettleston	Crew Jcn
J	22.05	Princes St	Carstairs	9	18.00	Carlisle	Lothian Rd
K	21.55	Crew Jcn	Dalzell	10	16.25	Liverpool	Princes St
L	22.55	Slateford	Mossend	11	21.25	Glasgow	Princes St
M	23.30	Princes St	B'ham				
N	23.40	Slateford	Polmadie				

Scotland was not overburdened with 5XP Jubilee 4-6-0's and in early 1955 there were only nine examples of the type shedded north of the border: six at Corkerhill and three at Perth. Most of the English visitors came from the eighteen engines allocated to Kingmoor and the appearance of Longsight-based 45632 'Tonga' on an excursion in February 1955 came as something of a surprise. It was a long established LM practice not to change engines en route if it could be helped and excursion trains into Edinburgh therefore brought with them some interesting visitors.

Train	00.15					07.33				09.12	09.30	10.55	10.55		12.20				10.30			13.25	14.00		
From	Granton					Stir'g				Stir'g	Call'r	Granton	Granton		Granton				Lth E.			Stir'g	DM		
Class	K	Milk	K	B	K	B	B	B	B	A	A	K	K	C	B	K	B	B	K	A	K	A	B	B	Milk
LEITH NORTH				07.25	07.30	07.56		08.27	08.54					11.55	12.05		12.38	13.02		13.43			14.30	15.06	
Newhaven				07.28		07.59		08.30	08.57						12.08		12.41	13.05		13.46			14.33	15.09	
Newhaven Jn					07/35									11/58											
Granton Road				07.31		08.02		08.33	09.00						12.11		12.44	13.08		13.49			14.36	15.12	
East Pilton				07.34		08.05		08.36	09.03						12.14		12.47	13.11		13.52			14.39	15.15	
Crew Jcn	00/25				07/40							11/03		12/04		12/28			13/20						
Craigleith				07.38		08.09		08.40	09.07			11.08	11.25		12.18		12.51	13.15		13.56		14.25	14.43	15.19	
Murrayfield				07.41		08.12		08.43	09.10				11.32		12.21		12.54	13.18		13.59			14.46	15.22	
Coltbridge Jn	00/33				07/46							11/32		12/10		12/33			13/28		14/30				
Haymarket W. Jn		01.05	05.25				08/34			10/08	10/59											14/19			16.20
Dalry Road	01/10		05/30	07.43		08.14	08.37	08.45	09.12	10/10	11/01			12/12	12.23		12.56	13.20		14.01		14/21	14.48	15.24	16/22
Morrison St Gds																12.40									
Lothian Road Gds			05.35											12.15											16.26
PRINCES STREET	01.15			07.46		08.17	08.40	08.48	09.15	10.12	11.03				12.26		12.59	13.23		14.04		14.23	14.51	15.27	
Dest		S'ford				S'ford				S'ford									S'ford			S'ford			

Train	01.40			06.15		06.35					08.25	08.35	08.35							12.55	12.55				13.20
From	S'ford			S'ford		S'ford					S'ford	S'ford	S'ford							S'ford	S'ford				M. St
Class	K	K	K	K	Milk	K	A	B	B	B	K	K	K	A	B	A	B	B	B	K	K	A	K	K	K
PRINCES STREET					03.15		06.50	07.20	07.57	08.22				09.25	11.34	11.40	11.58	12.36	12.57			13.15			
Lothian Road Gds		04.55	06.05																						
Morrison St Gds																							13.20	13.25	
Dalry Road		05/00	06/10		03/18		06.53	07.22	08.00	08.25				09/32	11.37	11/42	12.01	12.39	13.00			13/17	13/23	13/26	
Haymarket W. Jn		05.05			03.20		06.56							09/34		11/44									
Coltbridge Jn	01/46		06/13	06/20		06/43					08/32	08/40								13/04			13/25	13/28	
Murrayfield								07.26	08.02	08.27					11.39		12.03	12.41	13.02	13.08	13.20				
Craigleith								07.29	08.05	08.30					11.42		12.06	12.44	13.05						
Crew Jcn	01/52		06/20	06/30		06/50					08/40	08.48	09.05							13/25			13.30	13/35	13.45
East Pilton								07.31	08.08	08.31					11.45		12.09	12.47	13.08						
Granton Road								07.36	08.11	08.36					11.48		12.12	12.50	13.11						
Newhaven Jn			06/25			07.00							09/15												13/55
Newhaven								07.39	08.14	08.40					11.51		12.15	12.53	13.14						
LEITH NORTH			06.30					07.41	08.16	08.44			09.25		11.53		12.17	12.55	13.16						
Dest	Granton			Granton		L. East	Call'r				Granton			Perth		Stir'g				DM		Stir'g		Granton	Sea'd

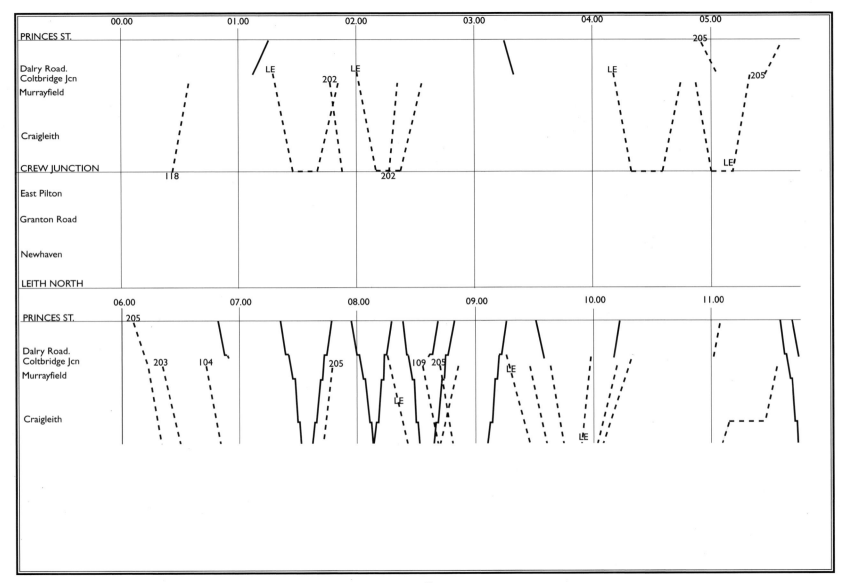

WORKING TIMETABLE (PASSENGER & GOODS) : 1955

Train		15.52							18.48		18.10	21.00
From		Lar'bt							Lar'bt		Leith	Stir'g
Class	B	A	B	B	B	F	B	K	A	K	K	A
LEITH NORTH	16.08		17.11	17.28	17.42	18.00	18.09	18.10			19.55	
Newhaven	16.11		17.14	17.31	17.45		18.12					
Newhaven Jn						18/05		18.15		19.20	20/00	21.20
Granton Road	16.14		17.17	17.34	17.48		18.15					
East Pilton	16.16		17.20	17.36	17.51		18.18					
Crew Jcn						18/10				19/28	20/05	21/28
Craigleith	16.22		17.23	17.42	17.55		18.22					
Murrayfield	16.25		17.29	17.45	17.58		18.25					
Coltbridge Jn						18/17				19/33	20/12	21/37
Haymarket W. Jn		16/30							19/27			21/54
Dalry Road	16.28	16.34	17.31	17.48	18.00		18.27		19.31			21/56
Morrison St Gds										19.40		
Lothian Road Gds												
PRINCES STREET	16.31	16.37	17.34	17.51	18.03		18.30		19.34			21.58
Dest						S'ford				S'ford	S'ford	

Train			14.55	15.15	14.55							17.10			18.45	18.45		
From			S'ford	S'ford	S'ford							L. East			S'ford	S'ford		
Class	B	B	K	K	K	B	A	B	B	B	B	K	B	B	K	K	K	A
PRINCES STREET	13.59	14.30				15.35	16.25	16.33	16.55	17.08	17.22		17.41	18.09				22.10
Lothian Road Gds																	20.10	
Morrison St Gds																		
Dalry Road	14.02	14.33				15.38	16/27	16.36	16.58	17.11	17.25		17.44	18.12			20/15	22/12
Haymarket W. Jn							16/29				17/28							22/14
Coltbridge Jn			15/00	15/20											18/52		20/17	
Murrayfield	14.04	14.35				15.40		16.38	17.00	17.13			17.46	18.14			Stir'g	
Craigleith	14.07	14.38				15.43		16.41	17.03	17.16			17.49	18.17				
Crew Jcn			15.10	15/25	15.35										18/56		20.25	
East Pilton	14.10	14.41				15.46		16.44	17.06	17.19			17.52	18.20				
Granton Road	14.13	14.44				15.49		16.47	17.09	17.22			17.55	18.23				
Newhaven Jn			15/35	15/40								17.35			19.05	19.15		
Newhaven	14.16	14.47				15.52		16.50	17.12	17.25			17.58	18.26				
LEITH NORTH	14.18	14.49			15.45	15.54		16.52	17.14	17.27		17.40	18.00	18.28	19.20			
Dest			L. East				Perth				Stir'g					Granton		Stir'g

TRAFFIC MOVEMENTS.

After the withdrawal of North British passenger services between Leith and Edinburgh Waverley in 1952, the Caledonian was able to boast of at least one strength in the Edinburgh area although its monopoly of the Leith workings was not something that was taken advantage of.

The steam service consisted of 15 trains in each direction but with some curious gaps. The service was pretty well suspended for three hours after the morning rush hour; the service resuming on a roughly hourly basis until six in the evening when the service ceased for the day.

Goods was the lifeblood of the Leith branch and the passenger service was therefore more of an irritation than a blessing in that it hampered the free movement of the many trips operating between the Docks and Slateford. It will be seen from the WTT and the traffic graphs that the margins between goods and passenger trains was quite tight. Targets 205 and 115 steered very close to the wind on one or two occasions.

Crew Junction - a source of train-planning confusion if ever there was one - was the marshalling yard for the Leith area although so far as it was possible traffic was moved direct from the Docks to either Slateford or Edinburgh. Iron ore traffic for the Glasgow and Motherwell area's tended to be tripped from the docks to Crew Junction where it was marshalled into block trainloads. The latter formed a fair proportion of Dalry Road's main line workings and necessitated a considerable mileage of light running between the shed and the MPD.

The volume of traffic was not inconsiderable and over the busiest section amounted to thirty passenger and fifty-seven goods or light engine movements.

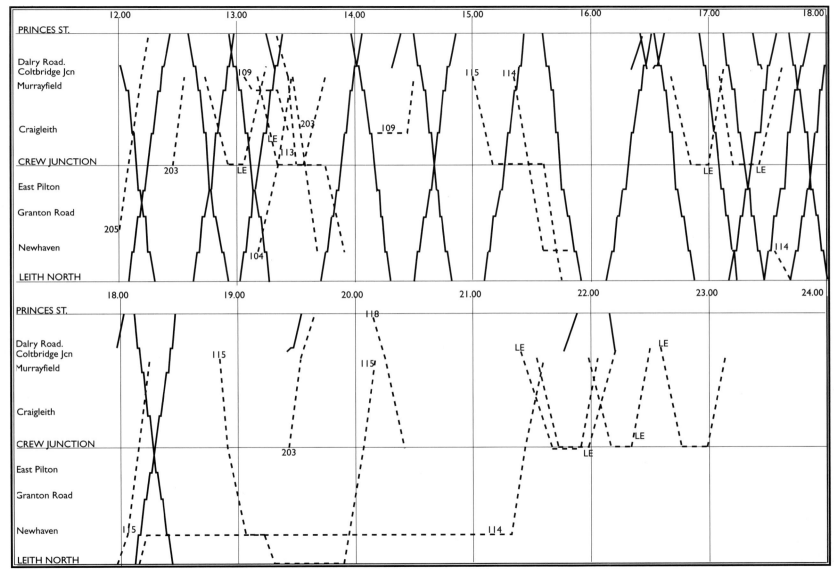

Another visitor to Edinburgh in February 1955 was 45599 'Bechuanaland', one of three 5XP's allocated to Preston and familiar to more southerly eyes as one of the regular engines for the 06.40 Euston to Windermere. The Preston engines were not fully utilised and were therefore often first choice for week-end excursion work. The pilot engine to Dolphinton Junction, Carstairs, is 4MT 2-6-4T 42695 of Dalry Road.

5XP 4-6-0 45604 'Ceylon' of Crewe North passes Balerno Junction on 6th February 1955 with a Rugby special for Birmingham.

the Glasgow main line, local passenger services were confined to the five and a half mile Leith North branch.

By suburban standards the Leith service was not especially intensive - fifteen trains a day in each direction - and finished rather early at night but it did provide enthusiasts with the opportunity to ride behind Caledonian '439' 0-4-4T's, half a dozen of which were allocated to Dalry Road shed. The Leith branch was also one of the last lines - if not the last - to perpetuate non-bogie stock and until 1949 many of its trains were formed of six-car sets of four-wheel non-corridors; stock that had been inherited from the Balerno branch.

With the North British controlling the northern corridor between Edinburgh and Glasgow, the Caledonian was unable to operate directly between Edinburgh and its territory north of the Clyde and the best it could manage was a rather half-hearted series of trains to Stirling using running powers over the North British via the mile-long spur between Dalry Road and Haymarket West Junction.

The service of seven daily trains survived until 1965 because it offered the most direct means of getting from Edinburgh to Stirling. It also gave the enthusiast the chance of riding behind an LMS locomotive over LNER mainline metals.

During the 1950's - and indeed at most points in their career - the Stirling services produced an interesting variety of motive power. Signalled as expresses, they were booked to be worked by class 4 locomotives, the actual engines employed varying from Dalry Road 4MT 2-6-4T's to D34 and Midland Compound 4-4-0's on the Perth-based turns.

Although passenger workings became a little lack-lustre after 1948, the volume of freight traffic remained high; much of the reason being due to the fact that the LMS penetration of Granton and Leith docks was little inferior to that of the North British and a constant supply of traffic was therefore guaranteed.

The principal marshalling yard was at Slateford which received traffic from both the main line and the docks to make up into services for Glasgow, Carstairs and Carlisle.

The greater part of the ordinary goods traffic arriving at Leith was destined for stations within Scotland and the tariff of services from Slateford tended to reflect this with four daily express services being operated to yards in the Glasgow area. With Glasgow being less that fifty miles distant there was no need to distinguish between fitted and unfitted traffic and all four services operated under rather a low classification; the accent being on volume rather than speed.

Traffic to England travelled much greater distances and of necessity had to be segregated. Two services were run to Carlisle from Slateford (20.00 fully fitted and 00.01 unfitted) with a third service running through to Carstairs from the docks but calling en route at Slateford to attach goods from Edinburgh.

A large amount of Norwegian iron-ore was imported through Leith for the iron and steel industries of Glasgow and to save tripping it into Slateford for it to be worked forward with a second engine, the ore was concentrated on Crew Junction, the point of divergence between the Granton and Leith dock branches, and worked as block trains direct to Motherwell or Glasgow.

These services - surprisingly unsung - were the very

For many years engines working in the Edinburgh and Glasgow districts of the Caledonian had been equipped with portable route indicators and these remained in use - theoretically mandatory for all trains except Anglo-Scottish workings - until the early 1960's. The indicators did not serve any particularly useful operating function and their use declined as the 1950's progressed. The above chart shows the indicator positions as they applied to trains arriving and leaving Edinburgh, Princes Street.

PRINCES ST : ANGLO - SCOTTISH DEPARTURES	
1935	1948
09.30 Manchester (V)/Liverpool (Ex)	10.10 Birmingham
10.00 Euston/Birmingham	10.50 Liverpool (Ex)/Manchester (Vic)
13.30 Euston	15.57 Liverpool (Ex)/Manchester (Vic)
14.00 M'ter (Ex)/L'pool Ex	17.40 Euston (Adv to Crewe)
16.30 M'ter (Ex)/L'pool Ex	22.05 Birmingham
17.50 Euston	
22.45 Euston/Piverpool L.St	

Class	LOCOMOTIVE ALLOCATION SUMMARY : EDINBURGH (DALRY ROAD).										
	Oct-50	Oct-51	Oct-52	Oct-53	Oct-54	Oct-55	Oct-56	Oct-57	Oct-58	Oct-59	Oct-60
5MT: B1 4-6-0 (1942)							2				4
5MT 4-6-0 (1934)	5	6	8	7	7	9	9	10	9	9	9
5MT 2-6-0 (1926)	3	3	3	3	3	1	1	1	1	1	1
5F: J39 0-6-0 (1926)									4	4	3
5F: J37 0-6-0 (1914)	2	3	3	2	2	2	6	6	2	3	3
4P 4-4-0 (1924)	3	3	3	3	2						
4MT 2-6-4T (1951)									1		
4MT 2-6-4T (1945)	6	6	6	6	6	7	7	6	4	2	1
3P: V1 2-6-2T (1930)											1
3P 4-4-0 (1920)	1		1	1	1	1	1	1	1	1	
3P 4-4-0 (1910)	2	2	2	2	2	1	1				
3F: N15 0-6-2T (1910)	1	1	1	1	1	1		1	1		
3F: J35 0-6-0 (1906)					2	4	4	4	2	3	3
3F 0-6-0T (1896)	4	4	4	4	4	4	4	4	3	2	2
3F 0-6-0 (1918)	1		1	1	1	1	1	1	1		
3F 0-6-0 (1899)	6	6	7	5	5	5	5	6	6	5	5
2P 0-4-4T (1900)	8	8	7	6	6	5	5	5	5	5	5
2P 0-4-4T (1895)	1	1									
2F: J36 0-6-0 (1888)	1	2	1								
2F 0-6-0T (1928)	1		1	1	1	1	1	1	1	1	1
0F: Diesel 0-6-0										5	5
0F: 0-4-0 Diesel											3

opposite of most mineral services which often had to be remarshalled several times in the course of a single trip.

The ore was unloaded at either Leith or Granton and the wagons tripped in small numbers to Crew Junction by dock shunter where complete trains were made up for Clyde's Mill works at Newton, the Clyde Iron Works at Rutherglen, Shettleston Iron Works or Dalzell Steel Works at Motherwell. Each destination was booked to receive two trains per day except for Clyde's Mill which had one. (The scale of operations connected with the Iron and Steel industry is difficult to overstate and, as an example, the Clyde works at Rutherglen received no less than twelve trains per day from a variety of locations bringing in raw materials of one sort or another).

Running on the outward leg under class J conditions (which sacrificed speed for tonnage), each Crew Junction train took approximately three and a half hours to reach its destination and, with a return load of empty wagons worked as a class F, about two and a half hours for the trip back to Crew Junction. Each working therefore nicely encompassed a turn of duty for the crew.

Most of the ore trains ran via Shotts in each direction but the two Dalzell services took advantage of Motherwell's position on the Carlisle - Perth route and inscribed a circular trip; the outward (loaded) leg being made over the Glasgow route whilst the return trip was made via the Caledonian mainline to Carstairs and thence via Cobbinshaw and Midcalder Junction. The circuit saved having to turn the engine at Dalzell and allowed Dalry Road enginemen to retain knowledge of the Motherwell - Carstairs section of line.

In January 1956 the solitary C (fully-fitted) working to Kingmoor was joined by a second class C which left Slateford at 18.40 and ran through to Stranraer via Johnstone. A corresponding train ran from Stranraer at 18.05 and both were worked by Dalry Road 5MT 4-6-0's.

A strange by-product of the Stranraer working was the arrival of a pair of B1 4-6-0's from St Margaret's for work on the Princes Street - Glasgow workings in order to release a pair of Black 5's for the Stranraer diagram.

Scotland was a major coal producing country and although the Midlothian collieries around Edinburgh were monopolised by the North British, Dalry Road had two trips which assisted with the clearance of the seven pits served by the branches at Benhar and Fauldhouse Junctions. Both points lay close to the boundary between the Glasgow and Edinburgh districts and most of the colliery output was dealt with by Motherwell shed who sent no less than eight engines to the area daily. (The incidence of 0-6-0's blasting uphill with empties from Bellside Junction, Cleland, to Benhar was sometimes such that as soon as one

---

MAIN LINE ENGINE DIAGRAMS - DALRY ROAD (64C) : 1955

DY 200 : N15 0-6-2T

arr	location	dep	
	Dalry Rd loco	00.50	Light
01.00	Lothian Rd	01.10	K
01.15	Slateford	01.30	K
01.35	Lothian Rd	04.55	K
05.05	Haymarket West	05.25	K
05.35	Lothian Rd	06.05	K
06.30	Leith North	07.30	K
07.55	Slateford	08.35	K
08.48	Crew Jcn	09.05	K
09.25	Leith North	11.55	C
12.15	Lothian Rd	14.55	K
15.10	Crew Jcn	15.35	K
15.45*	Leith North	18.00	F
18.25	Slateford	18.45	K
19.05	Newhaven Jcn	19.15	K
19.20	Leith North	19.55	K
20.20	Slateford	20.30	K
20.35	Lothian Rd	20.50	Light
21.00	Dalry Rd loco		

DY 202 3F 0-6-0

arr	location	dep	
	Dalry Rd loco	01.20	Light
01.30	Slateford	01.40	K
02.00	Granton High	02.30	K
02.30	Slateford	06.15	K
06.40	Granton High	06.40	K
12.40	Morriston St	13.25	K
13.45	Granton High	19.20	K
19.40	Morriston St	19.50	Light
19.55	Lothian Rd	20.10	K
20.40	Granton High	00.15	K
00.40	Slateford	00.45	Light
00.55	Dalry Rd loco		

DY 109

arr	location	dep	
	Dalry Rd loco	08.05	Light
08.15	Slateford	08.25	K
08.50	Granton High	10.55	K
11.08	Craigleith	11.25	K
11.40	Slateford	12.55	K
13.08	Murrayfield	13.20	K
13.30	Davidson's Main	14.00	K
14.10	Craigleith	14.25	K
14.35	Slateford	15.15	K
16.05	Leith East	17.10	K
17.40	Leith North	18.10	K
18.15	Newhaven Jcn	21.20	K
21.45	Slateford	21.50	Light
22.00	Dalry Rd loco		

DY 112 3F 0-6-0

arr	location	dep	
	Dalry Rd loco	08.55	Light
09.00	Slateford	09.05	K
10.11	West Calder	10.30	K
10.55	Woodmuir Jcn	11.00	K
11.20	Benhar Jcn	11.50	K
11.55	Fauldhouse	12.10	K
12.25	Woodmuir Jcn	14.30	K
14.52	Midcalder Jcn	15.12	K
15.27	Camps Jcn	15.32	K
15.38	Camps	16.00	K
16.05	Camps Jcn	16.15	K
16.35	Slateford	16.40	Light
16.50	Dalry Rd loco		

DY 104 3F 0-6-0T

arr	location	dep	
	Dalry Rd loco	06.15	Light
06.25	Slateford	06.35	K
06.35	Newhaven Jcn	07.20	K
08.00	Leith East	10.30	K
10.45	Seafield		
	Trips as required		
	Granton High	13.20	K
13.40	Slateford	13.50	Light
14.00	Dalry Rd loco		

DY 111 2F 0-6-0T

arr	location	dep	
	Dalry Rd loco	10.35	Light
10.40	Slateford	11.05	K
11.25	Currie	11.50	K
11.53	Kinleith Mill	12.03	K
12.41	Colinton	13.00	K
13.23	Balerno	13.43	K
13.48	Ravelrig Jcn	14.08	K
14.13	Balerno	14.23	K
14.33	Currie	14.38	K
15.35	Slateford	15.40	Light
15.45	Dalry Rd loco		

DY 113 3F 0-6-0T

arr	location	dep	
	Dalry Rd loco	13.00	Light
13.10	Morrison St	13.20	K
13.30	Crew Jcn	13.45	K
14.10	Seafield	14.20	Light
14.30	Lothian Road	15.05	K
15.10	Slateford	15.50	K
16.00	Lothian Rd	17.00	K
17.40	Lothian Rd	18.42	K
18.47	Slateford	19.02	K
19.10	Lothian Rd	20.00	K
20.07	Slateford	20.15	Light
20.20	Dalry Rd loco		

DY 105 3F 0-6-0

arr	location	dep	
	Dalry Rd loco	07.00	Light
07.10	Slateford	07.15	K
08.20	West Calder	09.15	K
09.30	Woodmuir Jcn	10.00	K
13.00	Midcalder	13.50	K
14.15	Slateford	14.20	Light
14.30	Dalry Rd loco		

MAIN LINE ENGINE DIAGRAMS - DALRY ROAD (64C) : 1955

IRON ORE WORKINGS

DY 14 5MT 4-6-0

arr	location	dep	
	Dalry Rd loco	01.15	Light
01.25	Crew Jcn	01.40	J
04.55	Clyde Iron Works	05.05	Light
05.20	Strathclyde Jcn	06.40	F
09.36	Crew Jcn	09.45	Light
10.00	Dalry Rd loco		
13.20	Crew Jcn	13.35	J
17.03	Shettleton	19.10	F
21.45	Crew Jcn	22.00	
22.15	Dalry Rd loco		

DY 16 5MT 4-6-0

arr	location	dep	
	Dalry Rd loco	09.30	Light
09.40	Crew Jcn	10.00	J
12.50	Dalzell	15.00	F
17.12	Crew Jcn	17.20	Light
17.30	Dalry Rd loco		
21.40	Crew Jcn	21.55	J
00.55	Dalzell	02.55	F
05.00	Crew Jcn	05.10	Light
05.20	Dalry Rd loco		

DY 3 5MT 4-6-0

arr	location	dep	
	Dalry Rd loco	04.05	Light
04.15	Crew Jcn	04.35	J
07.55	Clyde Iron Works	10.00	F
12.55	Crew Jcn	13.05	Light
13.15	Dalry Rd loco		

DY 4 5MT 4-6-0

arr	location	dep	
	Dalry Rd loco	02.00	Light
02.10	Crew Jcn	02.23	J
05.45	Clyde's Mill	07.15	E
09.45	Crew Jcn	10.00	Light
10.10	Dalry Rd loco		

EXPRESS GOODS WORKINGS

DY 24 5MT 4-6-0

arr	location	dep	
	Dalry Rd loco	21.15	Light
21.25	Slateford	21.38	E
	Buchanan Street	02.15	E
04.30	Lothian Rd	04.40	Light
04.45	Dalry Rd loco		

DY 20 5MT 2-6-0

arr	location	dep	
	Dalry Rd loco	19.30	Light
19.40	Slateford	20.00	C
22.51	Carlisle (K)	23.00	Light
23.10	Kingmoor loco	02.00	Light
02.10	Carlisle (K)	02.35	D
06.40	Lothian Rd	06.50	Light
07.00	Dalry Rd loco		

DY21 5MT 2-6-0

arr	location	dep	
	Dalry Rd loco	23.40	Light
23.50	Slateford	00.01	E
04.40	Carlisle (K)	04.45	Light
05.40	Kingmoor loco	05.30	Light
05.40	Viaduct Yard	05.45	E
09.40	Lothian Road	09.45	Light
09.50	Dalry Rd loco		

DY22 5F J37 0-6-0

arr	location	dep	
22.45	Slateford	22.55	F
00.50	Mossend	03.30	H
05.38	Slateford	05.45	Light
05.55	Dalry Rd loco		

DY 1 5F J37 0-6-0

arr	location	dep	
	Dalry Rd loco	00.30	Light
00.40	Slateford	00.50	H
02.55	Mossend	04.20	H
07.10	Slateford	07.15	Light
07.20	Dalry Rd loco		

DY 23 5MT 4-6-0

arr	location	dep	
	Dalry Rd loco	23.20	Light
23.30	Slateford	23.40	H
02.40	Polmadie	02.40	Light
02.50	Polmadie	04.45	Light
04.55	Bridgeton	05.10	F
07.25	Slateford	07.30	Light
07.40	Dalry Rd loco		

had passed out of earshot, another came in. At times there was scarcely room for passenger trains).

Motherwell was too remote for its shed to look after Edinburgh's needs and therefore a pair of Dalry Road trips, Targets 105 and 112, were booked to run with empties from Slateford to Woodmuir and Benhar respectively and to return with coal for Morrison Street and the outlying stations of Edinburgh.

Colliery activity was also found on the Midcalder - Carstairs section which had three pits on the Wilsontown branch. The servicing of these pits was performed by a pair of Carstairs-based workings - Targets 110 and 116 - which worked on an early and late turn basis. The method of working was for 110 to arrive at Wilsontown with a train of empties from Carstairs, the empties then being tripped and exchanged for loaded traffic at Kingshill, Climpy and Wilsontown collieries in rotation; loaded wagons being recessed at Wilsontown until the end of the shift when 110 would make them up into a train and work it forward to Carstairs, passing 116 en route. The latter would repeat the operation but worked its loaded traffic through to Law Junction before returning light to Carstairs loco at the end of its shift.

Carstairs shed operated a third trip on Mondays, Wednesdays and Fridays when Target 107 worked the wayside stations on the main line as far as Harburn, running round at Camps Junction before returning to Carstairs. On the days that it did not run to Camps, Target 107 worked a local goods up the Caledonian main line to Elvanfoot.

The 6-mile Balerno branch, which paralleled the main line from Balerno Junction to Ravelrig Junction, was a route fast disappearing from public consciousness by the mid-1950's. It was reputed to have been the last line for which four-wheel passenger coaches had been built (1922) but had lost its passenger

service in 1943. Surprisingly the four-wheelers survived the closure - during the war passenger stock was at a premium - and spent the following seven years working between Princes Street and Leith. Movements on the Balerno route in the meantime had declined from quite a frequent passenger service to a single daily appearance by (usually) 0-6-0T 47163 with Target 111 which spent about four hours a day servicing the several quarries and paper mills that were located on the branch. In 1946 a proposal to reinstate the Balerno passenger services using a push & pull unit was considered but in the event nothing materialised and the branch remained as a goods-only line until its closure in 1967.

Goods traffic in Edinburgh was dealt with at Morrison Street (coal) and Lothian Road; the latter being the principal goods terminus for ex-LMS flows of traffic with three trains per day from Carlisle and one from Buchanan Street, Glasgow, arriving during the night and

The Caledonian perspective of the Edinburgh district with all other lines being excluded from the map. In spite of this it does not take an intimate knowledge of Scottish railway geography to see how effectively the North British prevented its rival from gaining direct access to Central and Northern Scotland. The district boundaries were at Fauldhouse on the Glasgow road and Auchengray on the Carstairs.

early morning. There were no through workings in the reverse direction and instead loaded vehicles were tripped by a series of afternoon departures (chiefly by Targets 113 and 202) to Slateford where they were shunted into the evening long-distance departures.

Notwithstanding the occasional appearances of Pacifics in Princes Street, the fact that most trains ran behind small to medium-range standard LMS locomotives acted as a deterrent to visitors especially as the chances of seeing something impressive were guaranteed on an hourly basis at the adjacent Waverley station. Had it not been for the proximity of the North British no doubt Princes Street would have featured more prominently in the railway press: as it was, the station lived and died almost unnoticed.

The end of the Caledonian in Edinburgh as an entity virtually independent of the North British came in mid-March 1959 when a spur was completed connecting Slateford with the NB Edinburgh suburban line at Craiglockhart. The goal was to allow Caledonian goods services to reach Niddrie (and, later, Millerhill) Marshalling Yard and eliminate much of the work done at Slateford. Ironically the first train to use the connection was J36 64963 with a Slateford - Granton (NBR) goods demonstrating thus that the new connection also threatened a considerable amount of local activity.

This, combined with the general decline in dock traffic during the 1960's, eventually spelled the end of Caledonian activities in the Edinburgh dock area.

Several blows of the axe came during the 1960's. The Leith service - in spite of its multiple units - ceased in April 1962 whilst the Stirling trains decamped to the Waverley two years later. The end came in September 1965 when Princes Street closed with its surviving passenger services being diverted to Waverley.

Caledonian 0-4-4T 55124 of Dumfries revives memories of passenger services at Wilsontown with an enthusiasts special in 1954. The Auchengray - Wilsontown branch was situated in as remote a spot as one could find yet the LMS gave it a service of six trains in each direction which, given the negligible population of the area, was probably on the generous side. Unfortunately the train service gave connections to Carstairs and had difficulty competing with the post-war buses which ran direct to Lanark. Because of this the branch passenger service ceased in September 1951 although the collieries on the line continued to be served by a pair of daily trip workings from Carstairs.

Murrayfield Rugby specials excepted, the best chance of seeing foreign express engines came when the 10.10 and 10.50 departures ran as independent trains - as they often did during the summer - to Birmingham and Manchester as opposed to being attached to a Glasgow service at Symington. On the 8th June 1952 5XP 4-6-0 45577 'Bengal' of Kingmoor backs up to the 10.50 through train for Manchester.

The LM penchant for complex cyclic diagrams extended to the Leith branch where the 16.33 Princes Street to Leith was worked by a Polmadie 5MT 4-6-0 between arriving with the 12.19 Glasgow - Edinburgh and departing with the 18.12 Edinburgh - Glasgow.   The engine in the diagram on 7th February 1955 was BR Standard 4-6-0 73075 in its first month of service.

BR Standard 5MT 4-6-0's 73055 and 73057, both of Polmadie, pull away from Murrayfield on Saturday 26 February 1955 with a Special for Glasgow Central. The Standard 5MT arrived at Polmadie from mid-1954 and displaced the dozen-strong allocation of LMS 5MT 4-6-0's which were dispersed around the system. Very few Polmadie men thought the exchange a fair one.

BR Standard 4-6-0 restarts a Glasgow Central stopping train from Slateford on 30th October 1954. Although of no especial significance in passenger terms, Slateford played a major role in the freight work of the district, its marshalling yard being the point at which traffic from the Edinburgh goods stations and the docks at Leith was formed into main line services.

Standard 5MT 4-6-0 73061 of Polmadie approaches Slateford with a Glasgow Central - Princes Street stopping train on Saturday 26th February 1955.

From time to time LNER B1 4-6-0's - seemingly with a preference for named members of the class - were allocated to Dalry Road as an alternative to the indigenous Black 5. 61002 'Impala' and 61242 'Alexander Reith Gray' were based there during the summer of 1951 with 61246 'Lord Balfour of Burleigh' and 61407 arriving for a prolonged spell five years later.   In mid-1960 three more examples of the class, 61007 'Klipspringer', 61244 'Strang Steel' and 61260 were also allocated to Dalry Road.   Eight years after leaving Dalry Road in March 1957 for Dunfermline, 61407 is seen approaching Edinburgh Waverley with a stopping train from the Perth direction.

Some of the older drivers would savage their firemen for firing during the initial stages of a journey but with his train nicely on the move the fireman of 44701 (Carstairs) starts to place 'a little round the edges' as his train passes Balerno Junction, two and a half miles from Edinburgh.

The merging of the LMS and LNER into a single region gave footplatemen the freedom to apply for vacancies at any depot in Scotland and for this reason LNER engines became accepted more easily at LMS sheds than was the case in England.   The use of the powerful (5F) North British J37 0-6-0's on parts of the Caledonian was one outcome of the merger: 64634 of Dundee drawing forward to ring off Carstairs loco for the 08.18 class H goods to Perth North.   The engine had worked in during the night on the 22.40 Perth South class E to Law Junction .   The Dalry Road J37's were regular performers on the Slateford - Mossend (Glasgow) night express goods workings

J37 0-6-0 64536 moved to Dalry Road from Perth in early 1950 and remained there until September 1958 when it was exchanged with a J39 0-6-0 and transferred to St Margaret's. The engine is seen on 15th April 1949 passing its then home station with an up goods from the Aberdeen direction.

Black 5 4-6-0 44955 of Carstairs pauses at Carnwath with the 17.35 Princes Street to Symington. By all appearances a local train, the 17.35 actually qualified as an Anglo-Scottish train since the rear pair of vehicles were transferred at Symington to the 17.40 Glasgow Central and ran through to Euston arriving at 05.05 the following morning. The facility was cloaked in anonymity since the Edinburgh coaches were advertised as running to Crewe only. The coaches returned in the down Mid-day Scot from Euston to Glasgow, the last leg being completed in a Glasgow - Edinburgh service.

29th of August 1951 and the sulphur and hot oil can almost be tasted. 44952 of Carstairs comes to a stand after turning on the angle between Dalry Road and Slateford and waits for the stock of the 10.50 Edinburgh to Manchester to be brought in. The 5MT will work the train as far as Symington. In the background 2-6-4T 42270 of Dalry Road prepares to work the 11.34 to Leith.

Under normal circumstances passenger activity at Leith was limited to fourteen Edinburgh Princes Street suburban workings. This state of affairs altered considerably when major Rugby events were held at Murrayfield, the second station out from Edinburgh on the Leith branch. On these occasions full-blown express services of ten coaches and more would decant their passengers at Princes Street and then proceed as empty stock to Leith, four miles distant, where they would be prepared for their return workings. Signalboxes and other strategic points were well attended by traffic and motive power inspectors to ensure that everything went as closely to plan as possible. In the view to the left, on 26th February 1955 BR standard 4-6-0's 73059 and 73060 wait for the right away with one train of Murrayfield stock while 73055 and 73057 wait with another. Both trains were for the Glasgow area and all four locomotives were based at Polmadie. Visually it made a considerable change from the humdrum Caledonian 0-4-4 tanks which normally worked most of the passenger traffic on the branch.

Not the least of the operational difficulties in the Edinburgh District was the 1 in 161 gradient from Kingsknowe to Midcalder Junction and although 3 or 4-coach stopping trains could be handled by unassisted class 4 engines, heavy and fast trains needed special measures such as that demonstrated by Jubilee 45724 'Warspite' and Black 5 44827 as they accelerate a return excursion past Balerno Junction on 6th February 1955. The combined power of both engines were needed in order to maintain express speeds on the climb; an output of around 1200 dbhp being needed to maintain 45 mph with a 12-coach train on the climb to Midcalder.

One would give a lot to know what the Dalry Road crew made of K3 2-6-0 61897, seen passing Merchiston in April 1955. The Jazzers were very powerful engines - class 6 for goods purposes - and, once the crew had accustomed themselves to the LNER controls, would give a very good account of themselves going uphill. But downhill............the best advice was to hang on for dear life.

4MT 2-6-4T 42270 of Dalry Road pilots Edge Hill 7P Rebuilt Royal Scot 4-6-0 46123 'Royal Irish Fusilier' on the 09.35 Edinburgh to Birmingham (New Street) on Sunday 6th February 1955. The train has been strengthened - thus the pilot - because of heavy Saturday rugby traffic at Murrayfield. The pair are seen passing Balerno Junction.

To the writer's mind, the highpoint of class 4 development was the LMS 4MT 2-6-4T which was equally at home on tightly timed surburban work or rural stopping passenger. 42268 of Dalry Road pulls away from Carnwath in July 1952 with the 13.18 Edinburgh (Princes Street) to Lanark. 42268 was one of the first of the Dalry Road 2-6-4T's to be made redundant by diesel multiple-units and was transferred with 42695 to Polmadie in July 1959.

North British connections between Edinburgh Waverley and Stirling were poor and a better service was given by the ex-LMS trains which ran from Princes Street but used the North British main line between Haymarket and Falkirk Grahamston. The seven daily workings were shared between Dalry Road and Stirling sheds; one of the latters' Compound 4-4-0's being seen with the 17.22 Princes Street to Stirling near Haymarket West Junction on April 4th 1955.

The 3F J35 0-6-0's were introduced at St Margaret's in late 1952 as replacements for Caledonian 3F 0-6-0's. 64527 was the fourth of the class to be transferred, arriving in May 1954 and remaining there for the rest of the decade. It is seen passing Murrayfield with a trip from Leith to Slateford in 1955.

With the blurring of the LMS/LNER boundaries in post-1948 Scotland, Dalry Road, which had previously been a subordinate of Motherwell, was placed under the jurisdiction of the North British shed at St Margaret's. One of the benefits of the arrangement was to give Dalry Road quick access to a large pool of replacement engines whenever necessary which is how LMS 2MT 2-6-0 46462 came to be used on Target 109 - seen at Craigleith with the 12.55 goods from Slateford to Davidson's Main - on the 7th May 1955. There was a certain irony in an LMS locomotive being allocated to an LNER shed and then being lent out to an LMS shed.

Heavy traffic at Murrayfield station which served an adjacent sports stadium sometimes resulted in the strengthening of the Edinburgh - Leith services and their motive power being raised from the normal 2P 0-4-4T to something more powerful such as Caledonian 3F 0-6-0 57576 which is seen with a branch train near Craigleith. A survivor of the '812' class of 1899, 57576 still had a number of adventures in front of it when photographed in February 1955. Three months later it was transferred to Oban for the summer season and in April 1959 it and classmate 57679 were exchanged for a pair of J35 0-6-0's, finishing their days at Stirling.

Still doing the job for which it had been designed 54 years earlier. Caledonian '812' 0-6-0 57682 of Carstairs blasts its way through Carnwath with Target 107, the 10.45 Carstairs to Camps Junction, on 15th July 1953.

...and a short while later a Leith train of more conventional length came by, worked by a more conventional engine: Caledonian 2P 0-4-4T 55202. For a system with so many sharp inclines, one might have expected a preference for something like a GN 0-6-2T for suburban work but the Caledonian was very keen on the 0-4-4T and constructed no less than one hundred and sixty examples between 1884 and 1925. At the time of the photograph, 9th April 1955, seventy-four were still at work.

For reasons forgotten, the stovepipe chimney enjoyed a brief era of postwar popularity - in certain quarters at least - as it appeared on East Coast Pacifics, Austerity mineral engines and most of the Caledonian 0-4-4 tanks. The A1 and A2 Pacifics were very quickly given more handsome lipped chimneys but the stovepipe remained a permanent fixture on most of the 0-4-4T's. 55210, seen near Murrayfield on the 9th April 1955, was one of the exceptions.

On a bitter February 1955 day, 0-4-4T 55233 with steam appearing from many places it shouldn't, heads a passenger train on the Leith branch. This particular engine had been engaged on the Beattock - Moffat branch until September 1950 when it returned to Dalry Road to spend its final decade working between Edinburgh and Leith.